Lisa Fey
Project Manager

P.O. Drawer 1734, Atlanta, GA 30301
404 676-0023 Fax 404 676-8307
E-Mail: lfey@na.ko.com

PETRETTI'S
COCA-COLA COLLECTIBLES
PRICE GUIDE

By
Allan Petretti

PUBLICATIONS, INC.

21 South Lake Drive, Hackensack, New Jersey 07601

Acknowledgments

I wish to express my gratitude to the many people who call and write to let me know how much they enjoy this Price Guide. The hard work that goes into this book is softened by this out poring of support. I would also like to thank my friends, many of whom are listed below who helped make this book possible.

Sharon & Joe Happle	John Diele	Jay & Joan Millman	Dr. & Mrs. Eugene Brinker
Bert Hansen	Ron Paradoski	Bill & Jan Schmidt	Jeff Wright
Margaret Almond	John Morgerson	Robert E. Cox	Irv & Dot Shirey
Gordon Breslow	Dave & Melba Caldwell	Bill & Kay Hendricks	Larry Schulz
Thaddeous Krom	Jeff Brady	Chuck Fetterman	James McDonald
Freddy Brewer	Bob Nance	Don & Donna Arnold	Robert Rentzer

With Special Thanks To. . .

Thom & Frances Thompson

In every group of people there are always a couple that stands out, people who offer help long before you ask for it, and ask nothing in return. Thom and Frances are those people. Thom has been, since my very first effort my best critic and loyalist supporter. Thom & Frances have one of the finest collections in the country, including the most extensive Coca-Cola Chewing Gum collection that I have ever seen. Their collection and knowledge is available to me without question and I owe much of the completeness and extensive coverage in many areas of this book directly to Thom. There is truly no way to thank him for sharing his knowledge and research in the writing, editing and proofing of many sections of this book. But I'll try. . .Thom & Frances, Thanks.

Don & Marty Weinberger

Who allowed me to photograph some beautiful pieces from their extensive collection.

Dann & Jinx Perszyk

For supplying and always offering photos from their collection.

John Barbier

His time and energy on the ''magazine ad'' section of this book is much appreciated.

Jim Meehan

His expertise and help with the bottle section of this book was very helpful.

Randy Schaeffer & Bill Bateman

The C.C. Tray-ders (Randy & Bill) through their research and writings especially during their years producing ''The Coca-Cola Collectors News'' have brought forth more information about the history of Coca-Cola than all other sources put together.

Leonard J. and Joseph L. Schiff

Authors of ''Edward Payson Baird; Inventor, Industrialist, Enterpreneur'' for their help with the ''Baird Clock'' section of this book.

Gael & Rosalie deCourtivron

Their collection of toys is one of the best in the country and have always made it available to me. Their help in expanding this section of the book is much appreciated.

Joseph F. Rinaldi & Susan Anievas

The production and printing of this book could not have been done without the extensive effort of my partner Joe and Bindery Manager Susan who makes sure these books are put together properly. Along with all the staff at AJP Graphics, Inc. who produce a fine line of books on antiques and collectibles.

The Coca-Cola Company/Phillip F. Mooney, Archives Manager

For supplying me with photos for this book, and always extending an invitation from The Archives for any help I might need.

Pop Poppenheimer (1922–1988)

One of the best known collectors of Coca-Cola memorabilia passed away in 1988. Pop was so well liked among the collecting community that anyone who knew him will never forget him. . .He will be missed. Pop and his wife Belle were among the first to make their collection available to me for this book.

And to my wife Rannie and my three great children, Dante, Deana & Vito who tolerate the never ending phone calls and hours that go into this book. . .I Love You All

CONTENTS

CONTENTS

INTRODUCTION

With the tremendous success of The Coca-Cola Co. over the past 100 years, it was inevitable that there would be a keen interest, not only in studying the history of this great American company, but also tracing it's advertising through the years, because without it's great advertising, there would not be a great company.

That advertising has been so successful because it has attempted to reflect American life and values. There is no one who can deny that success and anyone who examines this advertising can certainly appreciate the beauty as well as the message it represents.

To me, it is much more than advertising. I truly see it as an art form that is "Americana" at it's best. It traces the style and fashions of American life from our "Victorian Era" to the present day, and as you examine the quality of the artwork and lithography that has become the trademark of this company, I'm sure you will share my passion for it. That passion is not only my own, but rather it is shared by thousands of people all over the world, who truly admire this great advertising.

Since the early 1970's, the interest in this advertising began to peak as collectors realized they weren't alone, and through antique publications they slowly came together as a group of people who study, appreciate and collect the memorabilia of The Coca-Cola Co. This interest has grown tremendously over these past years and especially since the company celebrated it's 100th Anniversary in 1986, and with that it becomes more evident that the need for a complete and up-to-date guide to the current monetary value of this much sought after memorabilia, is great.

Many price guides and reference books on the subject have been written since the early 1970's. While many of these books contained much information and some even paved the way for many of today's top collectors, some of that early information was erroneous and misleading, sometimes this was due to a lack of knowledge on the part of the authors. To this day these price guides are still produced and sold and remain a fixture in the collecting world. The prices and information, correct or otherwise, seems to go on forever. I personally don't believe in that type of price guide. This book is the sixth of a series which I began in the mid-1970's and will continue, as long as there is a need for it.

One thing that this book is **not** is a completely new volume. Forcing the reader, who owns a complete set of books, to always try to figure out what item is in what book. What this book **is**, is a completely new edition with all the same items plus many, many new pieces. This is a whole new compilation with a new price structure and changes and corrections that come to light over a period of two years, since the last edition. This book makes all other guides, including my own, obsolete. It is truly the "encyclopedia" of Coca-Cola collectibles.

I have not attempted to write the history of The Coca-Cola Company, that has been done many times before by authors much more knowledgeable on the subject. What I have attempted to do in this book is show the reader what is available to the collector of this beautiful advertising memorabilia. And maybe even more importantly, to give the reader an idea of the approximate value of this memorabilia.

What you will see between these covers is the most complete and accurately dated collection of Coca-Cola memorabilia ever assembled in one book. It is, however very important to understand that with all the material shown in this book, it's only a small percentage of the vast amount of advertising and production material produced by the company over the years. I do hope that you understand that it is virtually impossible to cover the subject completely. I have attempted to show a good representation, and in some cases complete collections, in most of the popular areas of collecting. Also, many rare and one of a kind pieces are shown in the hopes that as collectors, you will find an item that you have and be able to determine it's approximate value, or at the very least find a piece similar so you can get an idea of the value. Please do not assume that just because a piece you own is not shown in this book that it is a rare item. Many very common pieces have been left out as well as rare ones.

I have attempted to learn by the mistakes of my predecessors. You will find this book quite different from many earlier price guides, and much easier to use. Different types of items are kept in their own sections, trays, calendars, toys, signs, etc. So, looking for a particular item is very easy. It will be much quicker to flip a few pages rather than a few volumes, to find a piece. You will also find the date, size and any other information directly below or next to the photograph.

I have also attempted to give the reader any helpful information in the form of "boxed in" notes on any particular item or group of items that I think requires additional explanation. You will also find in many of the main areas of collecting, "introduction" pages which go into some background, which you should find helpful. One particular area which I'm very proud of is the definitive outline of "Coca-Cola Chewing Gum", made possible by my good friend, and the person who knows more about Coca-Cola gum than anyone I know, Thom Thompson. The accurate story of Coca-Cola gum has never been written before, so you will see it first in this book. Thanks to the years of research by Thom, who by the way helped me to correct and expand that section and others in the book.

In regards to price or value there are a few things to keep in mind that are very important. First of all anyone producing a book that features current prices must realize that they have a great responsibility. Many people truly don't understand the point of a price guide which, by the way, is right in the title **"price guide"** and that's all it is, a **"guide"**, simply meaning, it gives an average price for the item considering the item is in nice clean presentable condition of excellent or better, the same item in poor condition will be worth considerably less and one in "flawless", mint condition will be worth more. The prices quoted herein are just one man's opinion. Many will think that they are too low and others will think that they are too high. Which ever side you are on, I can only ask that you do not consider the prices shown in this book as "law". They are only offered to the reader as an approximate value. Some pieces will sell for much much higher and others will sell for less. Putting a very high price on an item in a book such as this, is certainly an injustice to all collectors.

It is unfortunate, but true, that many people do not consider condition when pricing a piece. Many dealers who don't collect, take the seriousness of condition much too lightly. Most collectors are very serious about this and every buying decision is based on condition. I do feel that "average price for average condition" approach of pricing is much more responsible. By conducting auctions dealing with Coca-Cola memorabilia, I feel that I have a handle on the current values, and while I certainly take into consideration auction prices, I really can't use that as "true market value". In many cases, a high price on a particular item is caused by two people who just got carried away with the excitement of the auction. In most cases, auction prices are higher than prices being asked at antique shows and between collectors. I prefer to take into consideration, not only those auction prices, but also, prices paid by the average collectors all over the country, by asking questions, reading numerous antique publications, and actually selling these pieces myself and knowing what's "hot" and what's not. That is how I determine price or value, and this is how the prices in this book are determined.

No matter what field of collecting it may be you will always find people so eager to build a collection or own a particular piece that they will pay any price for it. It happens every day with fine oil paintings, coins, baseball cards and of course, Coca-Cola memorabilia. While these prices may be a trend of increased interest and higher prices, they are only one aspect of the pricing system.

With Coca-Cola, as with any other collectible, we have areas that are very "hot" and then cool off. Certain areas of collecting have a sudden interest causing prices to go up. Very often, that interest will level off and so will prices. Some areas of collecting have enjoyed long lasting interest, like trays and calendars, but in any case, the interest in collecting Coca-Cola memorabilia in general is growing by leaps and bounds, and it certainly stands to reason that the more collectors get involved, the higher the prices will go.

You will notice that prices as a whole are up considerably since my last price guide. However many have stayed the same, and still others, although not many, actually went down. The leveling off and lowering prices indicate either a softening of the market in that particular area of collecting or a large number of one item has come into the market, making the piece hard to sell and in turn, the price drops. Keep in mind that the three things that determine value are age, availability and condition, not necessarily in that order.

I have made every attempt to date each and every item in this book correctly, however some items are difficult to date and other identical or similar pieces were used for a number of years, and in some cases my dates may be just good estimations. I, of course, have attempted to correct any pieces that have been dated incorrectly, either by myself or others, and have used "circa" dates when the exact date is not known.

ABOUT THE AUTHOR

To produce a book such as this, it would seem logical that the author should know a great deal about the memorabilia and market in which he is dealing. Allan Petretti has been a collector, dealer and auctioneer of Coca-Cola memorabilia since the early 1970's, and beginning in 1975, he started Nostalgia Publications, Inc., which not only publishes this price guide but also a mail-bid auction offering quality Coca-Cola and other soda memorabilia. This auction, published twice a year, has become known as one of the main sources of buying and selling Coca-Cola memorabilia. And since it began, Mr. Petretti has sold more than 40,000 pieces of Coca-Cola and other advertising collectibles.

Mr. Petretti has also visited and photographed some of the countries top collections and is in touch, on a regular basis, with most of the long time Coca-Cola collectors. Traveling around the country to shows and auctions to purchase pieces for his own collection, certainly gives him the day to day feel for current prices. But, of course, it would be silly to claim infallibility when dealing with such a fleeting thing as current prices. But, all things considered, it can be stated, with clear conscience that the prices suggested herein are the result of a best effort by this interested collector/dealer.

Correspondence from fellow collectors is always welcome, as well as any information on rare and unusual items. Write to:

Allan Petretti
21 South Lake Drive
Hackensack, New Jersey 07601

CALENDARS

It is not a coincidence that calendars appear first in this book. They have been, since my very first day as a collector of Coca-Cola memorabilia, my main interest. I would consider trading any tray or sign I owned for that one particular calendar that I needed. Everyone who collects and enjoys the advertising and production material of The Coca-Cola Co., even those who collect anything with that famous trademark, will admit that there is that one area of collecting that is most fascinating to them. Because of the beautiful artwork and colors along with the fact that they are rare, calendars have become the most important pieces in my collection.

Many people do not realize the importance of the calendar as a marketing tool prior to radio or television. Of course there were newspaper and magazine ads and signs which brought the product before the public eye, but the calendar was much more than that. This was a useful product that was given away to consumers with the hope that they would hang them in their houses, both to remind them of the date and that Coca-Cola was "delicious and refreshing". It obviously worked and worked well and The Coca-Cola Company realized this, producing at least one type of calendar every year beginning in 1891. In some cases a few different calendars were produced in one year.

During my early years of collecting there was only one group of price guides available

on Coca-Cola collectibles and the discrepancies between the calendars shown in these books and the calendars that I was purchasing was very obvious. It soon became clear that many of the calendar pads shown were switched or altered in some way. Those price guides, unfortunately, are still available, showing the misdated and altered calendars. With this book, I hope to clear up those discrepancies.

Prior to 1914, the sizes of calendars were not very consistent. I have made every attempt to give correct sizes whenever possible. The size of the complete calendar (including pad), made between 1914 and 1919, is approximately 13" × 32". And from 1920 to 1922, they measured 12" × 32". All of these calendars were equipped with a metal strip and hanger at the top. From 1923 to 1940, the size was approximately 12" × 24", again with metal strip and hanger. In 1926, however, the calendar changed drastically, measuring 10½" × 18⅝" and printed on a medium weight card stock, it had a hole drilled at the top for hanging (replacing the standard metal strip). 1926 was also the first year that the calendar had a cover sheet over the pad which simply said "1926 Compliments of The Coca-Cola Co., Atlanta, Ga." The standard use of cover sheets over the pad didn't start until after 1930.

Another interesting aspect of Coca-Cola calendars is the glass and bottle variations. Because of the obvious difference between fountain and bottle sales, two calendars were issued in certain years, one showing the model holding a glass and one holding a bottle. In some of these cases, one type of calendar

may be rarer than the other, depending on how many have turned up over the years. The following is a list of calendars that have been printed in two separate versions of glass and bottle: 1904, 1914, 1915, 1916, 1917, 1919 (knitting girl), 1920, 1923, and 1927. The bottle version of the 1923 calendar is very unusual in that the bottle is embossed "8 oz." rather than the standard "6½ oz." which is the size of the bottle used at that time. The 1927 calendar has a slightly different variation also. On one calendar, there is a large bottle inset with a border around it, on the lower left hand side and another with no bottle at all. There is also a glass variation on the 1928 distributor calendar. In 1918 and from 1921 to 1930, (with the exception of 1923 and 1927), calendars show both glass and bottle and from 1931 on they show bottles only.

As any collector, who actively seeks Coca-Cola calendars, knows, they are not easy to find. Anything prior to 1914 is considered rare and anything prior to 1910 is very rare. Despite the rarity of these early calendars though, if they are found without a pad or a sheet attached, or trimmed from their original size, the value drops drastically.

After 1940, there was a major change in Coca-Cola calendars. From 1941 through the 1960s, they were made as multiple page type calendars, usually consisting of six pages plus a cover sheet, with two months on each page.

The condition of the calendar, as with any other Coca-Cola collectible is most important in determining value. The prices you see on calendars in this book reflect examples in nice clean, presentable condition. Examples in poor condition or without a pad will certainly be worth less and mint untouched examples could certainly be worth more.

There are a few things to keep in mind when purchasing a calendar. First of all, be sure that it has not been trimmed from it's original size. (The measurement information provided earlier should be helpful.) The pad or sheet attached is also very important, make sure it is the correct year for the calendar. If it is not a full pad take note as to how many sheets are attached. One sheet attached (other than the last sheet) is acceptable as long as you realize that you are buying an altered calendar. If a calendar is trimmed or has a partial or no pad at all, or has been mounted to poster board, it can not be called mint.

In this section of the book, you will find the most complete collection of Coca-Cola calendars ever assembled, including stock calendars, foreign and small size "home" or "reference" calendars, all of which are very interesting. Very few calendars known to exist are absent from this publication. Whether you are a die hard calendar collector like myself or if you just happen to have a few in your collection, I hope you will agree with me that calendars are certainly the most beautiful of all Coca-Cola collectibles.

CALENDARS

NOTE: Pre-1900 calendars are considered very rare.

1891 . . . . $7,000.00

Photo Courtesy The Coca-Cola Co., Atlanta, Ga.

1892 . . . . $7,000.00

Photo Courtesy The Coca-Cola Co., Atlanta, Ga.

1898 7 3/8″X 13″ $5,000.00

Photo Courtesy Gordon Breslow

1897 without pad $1,750.00
with pad $6,000.00

Photo Courtesy The Coca-Cola Co., Atlanta, Ga.

CALENDARS

1899 7 3/8"X 13" $5,000.00

Photo Courtesy Gordon Breslow

1899 7¼"X 12¾" $5,000.00

Photo Courtesy Joe Happle

1899 7 3/8"X 13" $5,000.00

NOTE: All of these early calendars are considered very rare.

1900 7¼"X 12¾" $5,000.00

Photo Courtesy Bob Nance

1900 7¼"X 12¾" $5,000.00

1901 7 3/8"X 13" $2,000.00

Photos Courtesy The Coca-Cola Co., Atlanta, Ga.

CALENDARS

NOTE: All calendars prior to 1914 are considered rare. Calendars found without a pad or pages attached would be worth considerably less.

1903 7¾"X 15" $2,300.00

2 Different versions of the 1903 calendar exist. Above Copyright date 1902, to the right Copyright date 1901, with a logo variation.

1903 7¾"X 15" $2,300.00

1905 7¾"X 15¼" $2,750.00

1907 . . . . $2,750.00
Photo Courtesy The Coca-Cola Co., Atlanta, Ga.

1908 . . 7"x 14" . . $1,500.00
There is also a larger version of this calendar

1910 . . VERY RARE . . $2,500.00
Photo Courtesy The Coca-Cola Co., Atlanta, Ga.

CALENDARS

*NOTE: All of these early calendars
are considered rare.*

1899 7 3/8''X 13'' . . . $5,000.00

1901 7 5/8''X 11'' $3,500.00

1902 7½''X 14½'' . . $2,500.00

1903 7¾''X 15'' . . . $2,300.00

1904 7¾''X 15¼'' . . . $2,300.00

1906 7¾''X 15¼'' . . . $2,800.00

CALENDARS
(Hamilton King Art)

NOTE: Artist "Hamilton King" painted the very beautiful "Coca-Cola Girls" for the calendars from 1910 to 1913. All of this art work was used on trolley car signs for the same years.

1910 8¾''X 17½'' $2,000.00

1911 10½''X 17¾'' $1,750.00

1912 (large version)
12¼''X 30¾'' . . Rare $2,500.00

1912 (small version)
9¾''X 19¾'' $2,000.00

1913 13½''X 22½'' $1,750.00

CALENDARS
GLASS AND BOTTLE VARIATIONS

1914 . . . . $700.00

Photos Courtesy: Gordon Breslow

1914 with bottle . . . $1,200.00
VERY RARE

NOTE:
The bottle version of both the 1914 and 1915 calendars are considered very rare. Both required extensive "artwork alterations" to accommodate the bottle. Notice the complete re-positioning of arm and hand on the 1914 and lowering of the arm on the 1915.
In contrast the 1916, 1917, 1919, and 1920 required simply adding the bottle.

1915 with glass . . . $1,000.00

(There are two different color variations of the 1915 calendar. One logo is gray and red and another is all red.)

1915 with bottle . . . $1,500.00
VERY RARE

1916 with glass . . $650.00

1916 with bottle . . $650.00

NOTE:
It's interesting that while some variation calendars are rare, others like the 1916 and 1919 have turned up pretty much the same over the years.

CALENDARS
GLASS AND BOTTLE VARIATIONS

NOTE:
The artwork on the 1919 calendar is very interesting and colorful, it has always been very popular with collectors.
This has made it somewhat difficult to find. The glass and bottle variations seem to have turned up evenly over the years.

1917 with glass . . $900.00
RARE

1917 with bottle . . . $750.00

1919 with glass . . . $900.00

1919 with bottle . . . $900.00

1927 with glass . . . $475.00   1927 with glass and bottle . $375.00

NOTE:
The bottle version of the 1927 calendar is completly different from all other variations. The bottle version has also turned up more often over the years.

CALENDARS (DISTRIBUTOR AND SMALL SIZE)

1918 JUNE CAPRICE 5''X 9''
$125.00

1919 MARION DAVIS 8''X14'' . $500.00

1917 CONSTANCE 8''X19½'' $425.00

1916 MISS PEARL WHITE 8''X15'' . . . $500.00
(This calendar was a magazine insert piece.)

Regulation
Glass

1928 8''X14'' . . . . $385.00 Each
2 Different versions

Unmarked
Straight Side
Glass

1927 7''X 13'' $575.00
RARE

1914 . . $700.00

1915 . . $1,000.00

1916 . . $650.00

1917 Glass . . $900.00

1918 . . $1,200.00

1919 . . $900.00

1920 Glass . $800.00

1920 Bottle . $800.00

1921 . . $550.00

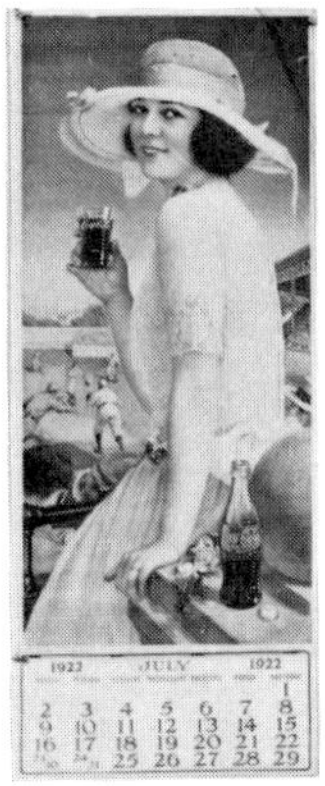

1922 . . $725.00

1923 Glass . $375.00

1923 Bottle . $375.00

1924 . . $450.00

1925 . . $400.00

1926 . . $525.00

1927 . . $375.00

1928 . . $450.00

1929 . . $575.00

1930. . $600.00

1931 . . $475.00

CALENDARS

1932 . . $300.00   1933 . . $300.00   1934 . . $300.00   1935 . . $350.00   1936 . . $325.00

1937 . . $250.00   1938 . . $200.00   1939 . . $175.00   1940 . . $150.00   1941 . . $85.00

1942 . . $75.00   1943 . . $70.00   1944 . . $70.00   1945 . . $70.00

1947 . . $60.00   1948 . . $60.00   1949 . . $60.00   1950 . . $60.00

CALENDARS

1951 . . $50.00

1952 . . $60.00

1953 . . $60.00

1954 . . $50.00

1955 . . $35.00

1957 . . $35.00

1958 . . $25.00

1959 . . $25.00

1960 . . $20.00

NOT PICTURED:
1961 . . $20.00
1965 . . $20.00

1963 . . $20.00

1964 . . $20.00

1967 . . $20.00

1968 . . $20.00

CALENDARS

1946 . . $100.00

1956 . . . $25.00

1966 . . . $20.00

1972 . . . $10.00

1973 Cloth . . . $10.00

1974 Cloth . . . $10.00

1975 . . . $5.00

1936 Distributor Calendar
Hamilton Bermuda
(Rolf Armstrong Art) . . $200.00

CANADIAN (FRENCH) CALENDARS

1941 . . . $125.00

1947 . . . $50.00

1948 . . . $50.00

1952 . . . $35.00

1955 . . . $35.00

1956 . . . $30.00

1958 . . . $30.00

1957 . . . $15.00

CALENDARS

1949 Local Bottler 19½"X 29" . . $75.00

1975 . . . $5.00

1976 . . . . $6.00

1980 . . . $5.00

1979 . . . $5.00

1978 . . . $5.00

1977 . . . . $5.00

1977 . . . $5.00

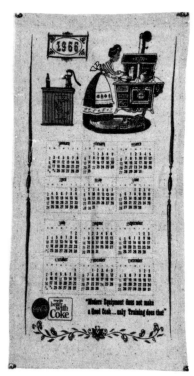

1966 cloth "Kitchen" calendar . . $25.00

1978 . . . $5.00

1980 . . . $5.00

1970 . . $5.00

1980 . . . . $5.00

1973. . . $8.00

1971 . . . $8.00

1979 . . . $5.00

1972 . . . $5.00

CALENDARS

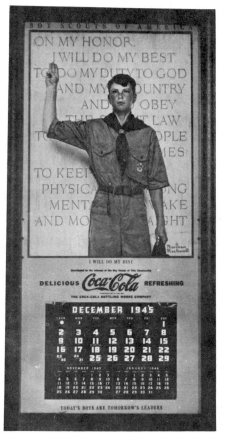

1945 . . . . $300.00

1946 . . . . $300.00

1953 . . . . $150.00

1944
MEXICO $250.00

1973 Houston Bottling Co.
Rockwell Art $25.00

1954 HONG KONG . . . $175.00

CALENDARS
HOME OR REFERENCE CALENDARS

1954 . . . $10.00

1955 . . . $10.00

1956 . . . $10.00

1957 . . . $10.00

1958 . . . $8.00

1959 . . . $8.00

1960 . . . $8.00

1961 . . . $8.00

1962 . . . $7.00

1963 . . . $7.00

1964 . . . $6.00

1965 . . . $6.00

1966 . . . $6.00

1967 . . . $5.00

1968 . . . $3.00

1969 . . . $3.00

1970 . . . $2.00

SERVING TRAYS

When I first started collecting the memorabilia of The Coca-Cola Company, the serving tray was the main point of interest. It seemed that everyone's collection was judged by which trays you had and which trays you needed. There has been a fascination with the tin lithographed serving tray ever since the first day people became interested in collecting Coca-Cola, and early price guides on the subject reflect this fact. While other items were shown, of course, the most important subject was the serving tray. Even The Coca-Cola Company archives produced in 1970 a book called "Catalog of Metal Service Trays and Art Plates Since 1898", which seems to be the first book on the subject, and in fact, Coca-Cola collecting in general.

While much has been learned since the 1970 book and other early price guides and reference books, one thing remains the same, the serving tray is still king. While many collectors could care less, I find that the main stream collector is still fascinated with the trays and many are trying for the seemingly impossible feat of owning every tray known to exist.

While it is quite possible that earlier trays do exist, the so-called 1897 "Victorian Girl" tray has always been thought of as the first and certainly the most important and most difficult of the trays.

Because of the importance of the tray, I think collectors have put more of an emphasis on the condition of trays, more so than other pieces. The typical tray collector considers every little scratch and dent on the tray. This is why it is so very hard for a book like this to place values on these trays and I must stress, once again, that the prices you see here are just **GUIDE** prices. In other words, what I call the average price considering a nice clean, presentable tray (excellent or better condition). If the tray is rough, the price will be lower and in some cases, of the more common trays, much lower. If the tray is in mint condition, it certainly can be higher. Please don't forget that just because a tray might have sold for a "fortune" at an auction, that certainly doesn't mean that that is the true market value. It is very possible that two people just got carried away with the moment.

The earliest known trays were basically 9¼" round made from 1897 through 1901. In 1903, there was also a 9¼" round tray but, another larger oval tray was used. In 1905, The Coca-Cola Company produced a smaller oval. This seemed to have continued until 1909 with a series of medium and larger oval trays. Tip or change trays vary in sizes from 4" to 6" circular types until 1907 when they became a standard 4¼" × 6" oval until 1920, at which time they were no longer produced.

Beginning in 1910, a rectangular tray was produced measuring 10½" × 13¼", which became standard and was used right into the early 1960's. Between 1910 and 1919 only three of these rectangular trays were produced, in 1910, 1913, and 1914. In 1916 a completely different tray was produced, it measured 8½" × 19", with no trays being made until after World War I. Then in 1920, they began to produce on a regular basis with at least one tray each year until 1942, and then not another until after World War II.

Most of these rectangular trays have turned up in sufficient numbers to keep collectors happy, however, most are always striving for that mint or, at least, near mint example, which is not always that easy. I have always been one who believes in the "upgrade" system of collecting which simply means, if you need a tray from a particular year, buy it even though it might not be in the most desirable condition and eventually, when you get it in better condition, you can sell the first one. Eventually your collection will be fine tuned to your liking. Sometimes waiting for that perfect example of a tray seems to take forever.

After World War II and into the 1950's and 1960's, the production of trays was, at best, spotty and irregular. T.V. trays, plastic and commemorative trays replaced the popular and beautiful Coca-Cola girls of the 1920's and 1930's.

Displaying trays has always been a minor problem with collectors. Everything from magnets, plate hangers, glue and string has been used, some successfully and others not. I personally think that the best way is a narrow shelf with an edge and simply leaning the tray on it. This works fine with no chance of falling. But which ever way you decide to display your trays, remember that taking care of them is much more important. The first and the most important thing is humidity. Do not store or display your trays in a humid spot, over a period of time the trays will become slightly pitted, and this pitting will eventually get worse. This presents a special problem for Coke collectors, many of whom, display their collection in game rooms or bars that are in the cellar. This could be a problem unless you have taken steps to reduce the humidity (a dehumidifier for example). The other big problem with trays is dust. It always seems to accumulate on the bottom rim of the tray. If this dust is allowed to build up, it will be difficult to clean and could certainly detract from the tray. If trays are not cleaned and dusted properly, you will get a series of light scratches. With all of this warning, I am trying to stress the fact that you must take care of your trays if you want to retain their value. Also remember that if you will be moving or storing trays, always put them into clear plastic bags. This is the best way to keep them from scratching.

So, whether you simply collect only particular trays that strike your fancy or you strive to own every example known, it is a fact that the tray is the classic Coca-Cola collectible.

1897 9¼'' $7,000.00

1899 9¼'' $6,500.00

NOTE: Remember the prices shown
on these early trays are based on
examples in excellent or better condition.
Trays in below average condition,
even rare examples, will not command a high price.

1903 15''X 18½'' $3,200.00

1903 9¼'' $3,000.00

1905 (with bottle)
10½''X 13'' . . . $1,800.00

1905 (with glass) 10½''X 13'' . . . $1,800.00

1900 9¼'' $3,750.00

1901 9¼'' $2,750.00

NOTE: Both 1903 "Bottle Trays" are considered rare and sought after by collectors. However, to warrant the prices listed below they must be in similar condition.

1903 "BOTTLE TRAY"
5½" Tip Tray . . . $3,200.00

Both "Bottle Trays" produced by Chas. W. Shonk Co. Litho, Chicago.

1903 "BOTTLE TRAY" 9¾" $4,500.00

c.1908 "TOPLESS" Vienna Art Plate
In original gold frame . . . $700.00
Without frame . . . $450.00

This plate found in the original shadow box, could add as much as 50% to the value.

c.1908 "TOPLESS" TRAY $2,400.00

Reverse side of art plate imprinted in center.

1913 . . . . $500.00
12½"X15¼"

1916 . . . . $200.00
8½"X19"

1906 . . . . $1,200.00
10½"X13¼"

1914 . . . . $400.00
12½"X15¼"

1907 . . . . $1,200.00
10½"X13¼"

1920 . . . $650.00
13¾"X 16½"

1909 . . . . $1,600.00
13½"X16½"

1909 . . . . $1,000.00
10¾"X13"

VIENNA ART PLATES

c.1908 - 1912

FRAMED PRICE
REFERS TO ORIGINAL
ORNATE GOLD FRAME.

PLATES FOUND IN
ORIGINAL GLASS
SHADOW BOX, COULD
ADD AS MUCH AS 50%
TO THE VALUE

Framed $325.00
Without Frame $150.00

REVERSE SIDE OF
ART PLATE
IMPRINTED IN CENTER

Framed $375.00
Without Frame $185.00

NOTE: These prices
are for plates in ex-
cellent or better con-
dition.
As that condition
goes down so does
the value.

Framed $375.00
Without Frame $185.00

Framed $375.00
Without Frame $185.00

RARE
Framed $500.00
Without Frame . $350.00

Framed $375.00
Without Frame $185.00

RARE
Framed $500.00
Without Frame $350.00

1900 6″ . . . $2,000.00   1901 6″ . . . . $1,300.00   1903 6″ $1,000.00

1903 4″ . . . . $750.00   1906 4″ . . . . . $400.00   1907 . . . . $385.00

1909 . . . . $275.00   1910 . . . . $275.00   1913 . . . . $250.00

1914 . . . . $200.00   1916 . . . . $125.00   1920 . . . . $250.00

SERVING TRAYS 10½"X13¼"
(The values on these trays are for good clean quality examples)

 1910 . . . $500.00

 1913 . . . $400.00

 1914 . . . $350.00

 1920 . . . $525.00

 1921 . . . $500.00

 1922 . . . $450.00

 1923 . . . $250.00

 1924 . . . $375.00

 1925 . . . $250.00

 1926 . . . $375.00

 1927 . . . $300.00

 1927 . . . $325.00

 1928 . . . $275.00

 1929 Glass $250.00

 1929 Bottle $300.00

 1930 . . . $175.00

 1930 . . . $200.00

 1931 . . . $425.00

 1932 . . . $300.00

 1933 . . . $275.00

 1934 . . . $450.00

 1935 . . . $185.00

 1936 . . . $165.00

 1937 . . $100.00

 1938 . . . $85.00

SERVING TRAYS 10½''X13¼''

1939 . . . $125.00   1940 . . . $125.00   1941 . . . $125.00   1942 . . . . $85.00   1948 . . . . $40.00

1950 . . . . $30.00   1957 . . . . $85.00   1957 . . . . $85.00   1957 . . . . $150.00   1957 . . . . $85.00

1961 . . . . $15.00   1972 . . . . $10.00   1975 . . . . $10.00   1975 . . . . $10.00

TV TRAYS 13½''X18¾''

1956 . . . . $10.00   1961 . . . . $15.00   1962 . . . . $15.00

1958 . . . . $45.00   1963 MEXICAN . . . $45.00   1969 MEXICAN . . . $45.00

SERVING TRAYS

1948 2 Different Versions
Solid Background . . $85.00   Screened Background . . $40.00

c.1959 "DRIVE IN" Tray . . . $100.00

1970's Mexican TV Trays
$15.00 Each

1958 . . . . $15.00   1970's Plastic . . $15.00

1975 Alabama/Auburn . . $8.00

NOTE: Additional recent, repro, and fantasy trays can be found on page 312

1961 "PANSEY GARDEN" 3 Different Versions . . . . $15.00 Each

TIP TRAY 4½"
Pre-1920 . . . $350.00

c.1940's. . . $375.00

c.1940's. . . $300.00

1953. . . $125.00

1954. . $100.00

1959. . $100.00

1961. . . $65.00

1961. . . $65.00

1963. . . $85.00

1965. . . $65.00

1965. . . $60.00

1966. . . $60.00

1968. . . $30.00

1969. . . $30.00

1970. . . $10.00

1971. . . $10.00

1972. . . $10.00

1973. . . $10.00

1974. . . $10.00

1976. . . $10.00

c.1896 CERAMIC SYRUP DISPENSER $3,000.00

NOTE: This syrup dispenser is 18'' high and consists of four pieces, lid, syrup bowl, base and brass spigot. Base and bowl are marked in a wreath ''The Wheeling Pottery Co.''.
It is considered rare to find this dispenser with the original brass spigot. Dispensers found without the original lid would be worth less.

LEADED GLASS CHANDELIER

1920's 18" CIRCULAR TIFFANY-TYPE LEADED GLASS CHANDELIER

(TWO DIFFERENT EXAMPLES)

$3,000.00 Each

1890's 10½'' ''The Ideal Brain Tonic'' $2,500.00

1901 8¼'' ''Hilda Clark'' . . . $1,500.00   c.1911 . . . . . . $700.00

CHINA

c.1930's Dinnerware individual pieces. . . . $125 Each   complete place setting $850.00

c.1930's 8¼'' Sandwich plate . . . Rare $350.00

1931 7¼'' Sandwich plate $125.00
(Manufactured by E.M. Knowles China Co.)

1931 7⅜'' Sandwich plate . . . Rare . . . $275.00
(Manufactured by American Chinaware Corp.)

1950's 50th Anniversary, Lenox china plate 10½'' . . . $150.00

1930's GREEN GLASS BOWL $175.00

1930's ALUMINUM "PRETZEL DISH" . . . $125.00

1967 GLASS "WORLD DISH" 11½"X11½" $50.00

1967 GLASS "WORLD DISH" 7¼" ROUND $60.00

COCA-COLA CHEWING GUM

The "Coca-Cola Gum Company" was chartered in Atlanta, Georgia, on March 17, 1903, by three Atlanta gentlemen. Their initial investment was $15,000. A contract was signed with The Coca-Cola Co. on March 23, 1903, allowing the use of the trademark, "Coca-Cola", on the chewing gum.

The company was very innovative, ordering vending machines as early as April of 1903. During the next couple of years some super Coca-Cola Gum related advertising was produced, including the bookmarks and a Hilda Clark cardboard poster.

It is assumed that Coca-Cola syrup was one of the ingredients of the chewing gum, as a 1904 ad states "contains the delightful tonic properties of Coca-Cola".

A group of Richmond, Virginia investors chartered a company named "Franklin Manufacturing Company" and bought all the machinery and assets of the "Coca-Cola Gum Co." of Atlanta on April 1, 1905. This new company relocated the business to 2405 E. Franklin Street in Richmond, Va. (A three story warehouse that had been a tobacco warehouse, and even served as a Confederate hospital during the Civil War. This building block today houses a paper and box manufacturing company.) The name of the company was undoubtedly derived from the address. In 1911, the name of the company was changed to "Franklin Caro Company, Inc." (Although the Inc. was omitted on most of the advertising) Most of the investors in the company were engaged in other businesses, and stock ownership and officers changed many times through the years. The company made a strong effort through the years to persuade Coca-Cola bottlers to sell the gum through their route men. Some ads appeared in "The Coca-Cola Bottler"

magazine promoting this. The gum was also carried by wholesale mail order grocers, and ads for the gum appeared in their catalogs. A few salesmen did call on retail accounts in the Richmond Va., Washington D.C., eastern Virginia and North Carolina areas, but the most extensive marketing was done, by mail, to the Coca-Cola bottlers.

In 1913, the business moved to 200 South Sixth Street in Richmond, Va., a four story brick warehouse building. (It is no longer standing.) From 1914 through 1916, the business prospered and the company added additional brands of gum to it's inventory. (until 1911, the only brand was the "Coca-Cola Pepsin Gum") "Caro Gum" was added in 1914, "Honeyfruit" in 1915, and "Richmint" in 1916. By 1912, they were also marketing different flavors of the "Coca-Cola Gum"; "Peppermint Pepsin", "Spearmint Pepsin" and "Wintergreen Pepsin" (Wrappers indicate the latter two were later labeled "Spearmint Flavor" and "Wintergreen Flavor".)

In December of 1912, the Franklin Caro Co. applied to the U.S. Patent Office, to register the trademark "Coca-Cola" as it applied to the chewing gum. When the application was published on November 3, 1914, The Coca-Cola Company immediately filed an opposition with the Patent Office.

On November 23, 1914, The Franklin Caro Company withdrew their application under threat of Coca-Cola not ratifying the original 1903 contract, which was still valid. The Coca-Cola Company continued with the opposition, when Franklin Caro Co., in early 1915, thought they might not have any trouble in registering the trademark, since they had used it for over ten years. The opposition was sustained and judgment rendered by the Patent Office in favor of The Coca-Cola Company on August 24, 1916.

However Franklin Caro Co., was successful in Registering the trademark "Coca-Cola" in Canada (Jan. 31, 1916) and in Newfoundland (Feb. 14, 1916).

In August of 1915, the principal stockholders wishing to sell the business, advised The Coca-Cola Co. of their intentions. Under a clause in the 1903 agreement, The Coca-Cola Co. retained the right of first refusal should a sale be contemplated. Negotiations with Harold Hirsch, council for Coca-Cola, and Sam Dobbs as a direct contact to Franklin Caro Co., carried on for nearly 9 months, before The Coca-Cola Co. finally tendered an offer of $7,000 on June 30, 1916, to buy the existing contract between the two companies. This offer was for the "Coca-Cola Gum" name only, not the physical assets. This offer was not accepted, and the gum company changed ownership again, this time through the influx of new investors into the business. Officers also changed at this time. The company was never on a sound financial basis after 1916. The war rationing hurt the business, and, with gum companies such as Wrigley's and Beechnut producing a better quality gum and using a more aggressive marketing and advertising campaign, the business continued to lose money. The "Franklin Caro Company" filed bankruptcy in early 1921.

In June of 1921, the company was reorganized under the name "Franklin-Caro Gum Company, Inc." The old company had been bought out of bankruptcy by a group of investors who were established in other lines of business. Another flavor of gum, "Velvet", was added in 1923, and the company added a line of roasted peanuts called "Smithfield" in late 1923. The company had made an attempt in these last years to improve the quality of it's gum by increasing the chicle content, but this was too little, too late. Sales decreased yearly, and records of sales showed practically no repeat orders of Coca-Cola Gum. The use of three flavors, under the Coca-Cola brand name, did little to help the market for the gum.

The Coca-Cola Company, after a couple months of negotiations, bought all the assets, stock, machinery, registrations, and contract for $20,000 in November of 1924, to prevent other firms from buying the company and actively using the "Coca-Cola" brand. In a memo to Robert Woodruff, it was stated that "no firm could use it more atrociously as to quality" than Franklin Caro had. The gum company was then liquidated.

The "Franklin Caro Gum Co." was succeeded by the "Smithfield Products Company, Inc.", which was owned by The Coca-Cola Co. and was chartered on January 20, 1925. They did continue to produce the roasted peanuts for some time. All of the chewing gum brand registrations were transferred to this company in the fall of 1925, but I have found no physical proof that Coca-Cola Gum was manufactured or marketed by them.

There is some evidence that "The Coca-Cola Co." considered marketing candy, cigars, and chewing gum with the Coca-Cola trademark on them in 1940. There is a pamphlet, although questionable, which depicts these products. Some of the gum wrappers as pictured in this pamphlet do exist. But, because of the war or some other reason, these products were never marketed at this time.

Rumor has it, and I have found some evidence to the fact that, The Coca-Cola Co. did sell "Coca-Cola Gum" periodically in small quantities after 1925. This was done to protect the registration of the Coca-Cola brand gum. But, for all practical purposes the gum was produced only from 1903 through 1924.

I want to offer a special thanks to Phil Mooney of The Coca-Cola Co. and Bill Ricketts, both of whom provided me with much of the information pertinent to putting this chronology together. Without their help, this could not have been written. (submitted by Thom Thompson, Versailles, Kentucky.)

c.1914 - 1916 "Dutch Girl"
Chewing Gum Cardboard Cutout
5¼" X 7¾" (counter display piece)
Very Rare $2,750.00

(Photo Courtesy: Thom Thompson, Versailles, Ky.)

c.1914 - 1916 "Dutch Boy" Chewing Gum Cardboard Cutout
(window display piece) 14" X 20½" . . . Very Rare $3,000.00

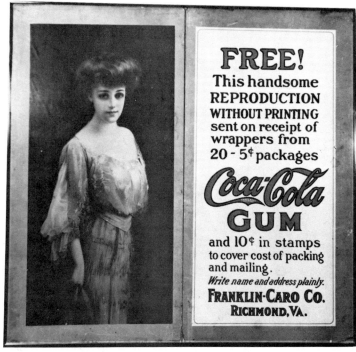

c.1908 Cardboard Sign
11" (Embossed gold corners
and wood grain border) . . . $2,200.00

Photo Courtesy: Jan Petry, Chicago, Ill.

c.1916 Coca-Cola Chewing Gum (Free Offer)
2 part window display piece, Rare $2,500.00

COCA-COLA CHEWING GUM JARS

c.1905-1911 Pepsin Gum Jar with paper label . . . . $1,100.00 with embossed lid add $100.00

c.1912 Franklin Caro Jar and lid (square corner jar) with Coca-Cola paper label $850.00

c.1912-1914 Franklin Caro jar and lid (bevel corner jar) with Coca-Cola paper label $850.00

c.1916-1924 Coca-Cola Chewing Gum Jar with Coca-Cola paper label $1,000.00

c.1912-1915 Coca-Cola Pepsin Gum Jar (bevel corners) . . . . . . $450.00 with embossed lid add . . $100.00 (square corner Pepsin Jar is earlier)

c.1916-1924 Coca-Cola Chewing Gum Jar . . . . $450.00 with embossed lid add . . $100.00

CHEWING GUM

Dates indicated are probable dates these particular wrapper designs were in use, based on information on letterhead and advertising. Few wrappers survive, being the disposable item they were. Beware, I have seen some wrappers reproduced by color xerographic means. Wrappers with original gum are worth more.

(photos courtesy: Thom Thompson)

c.1921-1924 gum and wrapper . . . $250.00

c.1903-1905 rolled piece of gum, for automatic gum dispenser. Gum and wrapper, 4½" $500.00

c.1916-1920 spearmint flavor wrapper $200.00

c.1913-1916 spearmint flavor wrapper $200.00

Prices to the Retail Trade

$3.15 a jar of 100 5c. packages.
.60 a box of 20 5c. packages.

At the prices indicated above, Coca-Cola Gum will show you a profit of more than 25%.

A reasonable supply of selling samples will be cheerfully furnished on request.

WIRE your order at our expense.

MADE BY
Franklin-Caro Gum Company, Inc.
RICHMOND, VIRGINIA

SPECIAL OFFER

· ON ·

Coca-Cola Chewing Gum

TO ALL BOTTLERS
OF Coca-Cola

BY
Franklin-Caro Gum Company, Inc.
RICHMOND, VIRGINIA

c.1921-1923 Price Card (folder) 6¼"X 6½" showing front and back $800.00
(prices and 3 sample pieces of gum)

c.1911-1913 spearmint pepsin wrapper $200.00

c.1913-1916 peppermint pepsin wrapper $200.00

c.1916-1920 peppermint pepsin wrapper $200.00

c.1921-1924 wintergreen flavor gum and wrapper . . $250.00

c.1940, 5 piece package wrapper, spearmint flavor gum . . . $75.00
(questionable that this was ever actually marketed, see preface).

c.1915-1924 honey fruit brand, 5 piece package wrapper . $200.00

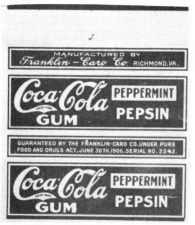

c.1916-1920 peppermint pepsin, 5 piece package wrapper . . $200.00

CHEWING GUM

c.1912 Shipping box cover wrap,
for box to hold 20 packages of gum $450.00

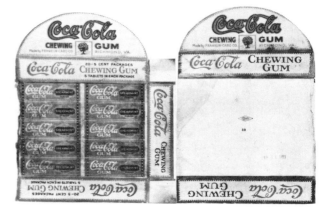

c.1920's Coca-Cola Chewing Gum counter display box
(box only) $450.00

c.1916 Cardboard shipping box, which held 20 packages
of gum (box only) $350.00

c.1920's Honey Fruit Chewing Gum
counter display box, product of
Franklin Caro Co.
(box only) $200.00

c.1925 Honey Fruit Gum
counter card $200.00

NOTE: This card shows the manufacturer to be Smithfield Products Co., Richmond, Va.

c.1903 - 1905 Porcelain sign, 7"X 8½"
This sign would have been attached above
and at back of the Doremus Automatic
Vending Machine, which dispensed the
rolled gum . . . . Rare $900.00

NOTE: Some of the Doremus machines came on the market in the mid 1970's with advertising etched on the glass. The machines and gum were (and are) authentic, but the advertising was added by a dealer of the period, attempting to enhance the value of machines he had for sale. This machine has been shown in a price guide with the spurious glass. These same machines were also used by cigar manufacturers in the early 1900's.

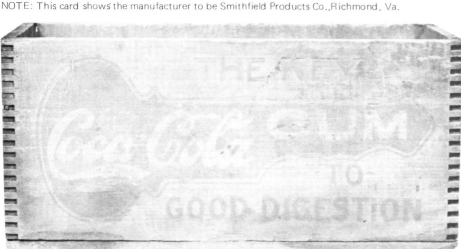

c.1913 Coca-Cola Chewing Gum wooden shipping box 12½"X 6¼" $200.00
These boxes were used to ship the glass counter display
jars, filled with 100 packages of gum.

-39-

CHEWING GUM

Photo Courtesy: John Barbier

Photo Courtesy: Dave and Melba Caldwell

Photo Courtesy: Thom Thompson

1904 Coca-Cola Chewing Gum,
Louisiana Purchase Exposition,
St. Louis, Mo. (Electricity Building)
Trade Card, Rare $500.00

Photo Courtesy: Thom Thompson

1903-1904 Coca-Cola Chewing Gum Bookmarks, 2"X 6" Rare . . . $600.00 Each

This fan pictures all children. A fan also exists picturing young women.

c.1912-1914
Chewing Gum Fan
Rare $1000.00

Photo Courtesy:
Phil Perdue
Louisville, Ky.

c.1912-1916
Chewing Gum Fan
Rare $1,000.00

Photo Courtesy:
Thad Krom
Maywood, NJ.

1921 Letterhead $125.00
(probable 1921 to 1924 usage)

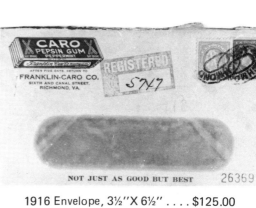

1916 Envelope, 3½"X 6½" $125.00
(pictures "Caro Pepsin Gum", one of the other
gum brands of The Franklin Caro Co.)

1908 Letterhead $125.00
(probable 1905 to 1911 usage)

1916 Letterhead $125.00
(probable 1912 to 1920 usage)

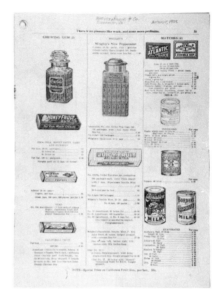

June 1918, "Harvey, Blair & Co." Wholesale Grocery Catalog
with page showing and pricing Coca-Cola gum $125.00

August 1922, "Harvey, Blair & Co."
Catalog (see left) $125.00

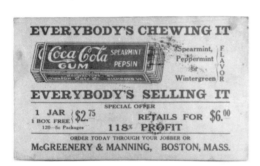

1912 "Special Offer" Postcard . . . $550.00

Photo's Courtesy: Thom Thompson, Versalles, Ky.

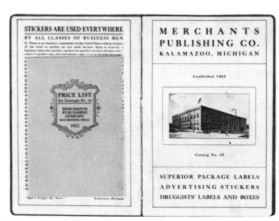

Spring 1919, "Southern Bargain House" Wholesale Department Store and Grocery Catalog,
with page showing and pricing Coca-Cola gum $150.00

1923 "Merchants Publishing Co." Catalog showing printed labels, including a "Coca-Cola Pepsin Chewing Gum" Jar Label
(this example would date from c.1912) hard bound book
and price list $125.00

CHEWING GUM

Very few ads for the Coca-Cola Chewing Gum exist. The only national distribution was that in "Everybody's Magazine". Each of those ads ran in several issues and are the most common of all gum collectibles. The other ads are of a more local distribution. All ads shown on this page appeared in black and white. (most photos courtesy: Thom Thompson)

1904 Ad, 1"X 2¾" "Everybody's Magazine" . $25.00

1906 and 1907
Ad, 1"X 2¾"
"Everybody's Magazine"
$20.00

Ad appearing in "The Coca-Cola Bottler",
October, 1912, 3½"X 4½" $50.00

Why Not
Chew ?

Ad from winter 1914-15 "Bijou Theater Programme"
Richmond, Va., 1½"X 5¼" $50.00

1905 Ad, 1"X 2¾"   "Everybody's Magazine" ... $20.00

Are You
Chewing   Or Are You
                                   Not Particular

Ad appearing on 1914 "Washington Nationals"
baseball score card, ad approx. 1½"X 6" $75.00

Ad from 1916 Richmond, Va.
City Directory, 5½"X 8" .. $100.00

Ad from 1907 "Guide to Richmond
and Vicinity" 3½"X 5½" ... $75.00

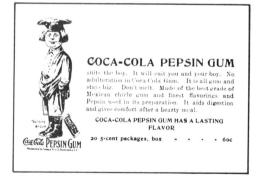

Ad from 1908 Peter Van Schaack & Sons,
Chicago, wholesale drug catalog .. $35.00

The Gum
Worth
Chewing   Everybody's
                                                  Chewing It
                                                  Try It and You
                                                  Will Like

Ad appearing in Feb. 1913 "Poli's Popular Players" program, Wash., D.C. 1½"X 6" ... $50.00

PAPER SIGNS

1910 "GIBSON GIRL" 20"X 30" $2,500.00
Has metal strip at top and bottom

1911 16" X 24" $2,200.00

1927 "BATHING BEAUTY" 20"X 32" . . $500.00

1921 20"X 32" $750.00

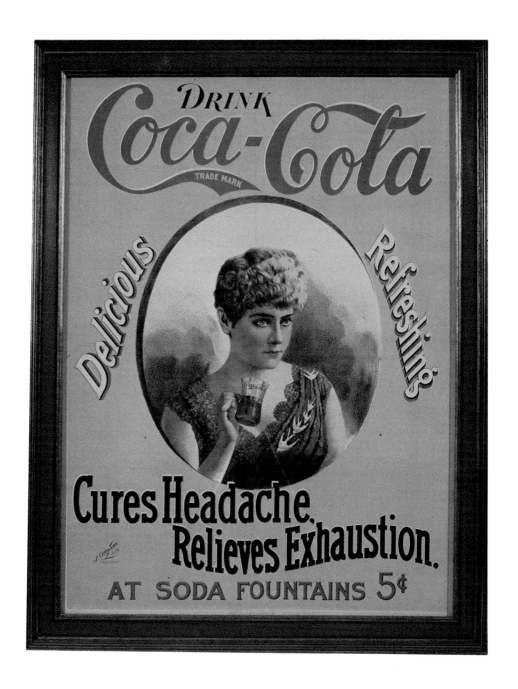

c.1895 CAMEO PAPER SIGN 30''X 40''
PRINTED BY J. OTTMANN LITHO, CO., N.Y.
$10,000.00

PRE-1900 PAPER SIGNS ARE VERY RARE

PAPER SIGNS

1901 "HILDA CLARK" 15"X 20" $3,000.00

1912 16"X 24" $2,000.00
(Printed by Ketterlinus Co., Phila.)

c.1912 16"X 22" $2,000.00
(Printed by Ketterlinus Co., Phila.)

1932 "Lupe Velez"
11"X 21½" $350.00

NOTE: Advertising with movie stars, celebrities, or sports personalities, as the subject matter would have more value than advertising showing an unidentified model.

1929 10"X 30" . . $275.00 Each
(Both have metal strip top and bottom)

1936 "Chinatown" 14½"X 22" . . $225.00

1920's Paper Hangers 12"X 20" (metal strip at top and bottom) . . . . $200.00 Each

PAPER BANNERS

1939 19"x 57" $75.00

1950's 13"x 41" $25.00

Late 50's 14"x 36" $15.00

1950's 18"x 60" $50.00

1937 19"x 58" $125.00

c.1920's 11¾" X 33½" $375.00

1940's . . . . $25.00 Each

1950's $10.00

1940's $15.00

1960's 19"x 57" $25.00

PAPER AND CARDBOARD SIGNS

Crepe paper
window decoration.
(used from rolls)

1950's Channel cards . . . . . . $8.00 Each

c.1927 10"X 16" piece . . . $50.00   1920's 10"X 16" piece . . . $35.00

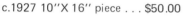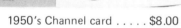

1950's Channel card $8.00

NOTE: A Channel Card
is a cardboard sign that
slides into a metal chan-
nel around the top of
the soda fountain.

1960's Channel card $5.00

1950's Channel cards . . . $15.00 Each

1950's Channel card
in wire hanger . . $10.00

HOT DOG

1930's Paper window
banners . . . $15.00 Each

1960's Channel card . . . $5.00

1950's 12"X 15" cardboard . . $10.00

1950's Channel cards . . . $5.00 Each

1950's 12"X 15" cardboard hanging signs . . . . $10.00 Each

-48-

PAPER SIGNS

1950's 11"X 22" $20.00

1949 11"X 22" . . . $35.00

1952 11"X 22" $20.00

1950's 11"X 24½" $20.00

1951 11"X 22" $25.00

1960's 13"X 22"
paper cutout $20.00

1950 11"X 24" $25.00

Late 1940's 36"X 52" (Amsterdam)
$125.00

1970's $15.00

1980 Marvel Comics / Coca-Cola 22"X 28" . . . . . . $10.00 Each

1953 Canadian (French)
paper cutout $25.00

TROLLEY SIGNS

Trolley cars, also called street cars, were first introduced in New York City in 1831. Originally, the trolleys were horse drawn carriages which operated on tracks in the street. As the end of the nineteenth century approached, most major American cities built street railways, but it was not until the electric street cars were introduced that the street railways came into widespread use. The first electric trolley was installed in Richmond, Virginia in 1887.

The electric street car, which was powered by electric wires above or below the street, revolutionized the American cities by providing the people with low cost, convenient transportation. Similarly, cable cars, introduced in San Francisco in 1873, were used

in hilly cities because they were thought to be safer in that type of situation. These cable cars were pulled along the tracks by an endless, engine driven, cable onto which the cars were attached.

By the turn of the century, the East and Midwest, with their expanded interurban service, had a street railway system larger than that of the railroad system. Unfortunately, mostly because of the ever growing popularity of the automobile, the railway system eventually began to decline and finally die. Now, cable cars can only be found in San Francisco and electric trolleys only in New Orleans. But, in their time, because of their low cost and convenience, the trolleys became a popular form of public transportation and therefore, an excellent place for companies such as Lucky Strike, Nabisco, and of course, The Coca-Cola Company to target their advertising.

This advertising came in the form of cardboard signs which collectors have dubbed ''street car signs'' or ''trolley car signs''. They are unmistakable because all are a standard size of 11″ × 20½″, printed on a lightweight, flexible cardboard. The size of these signs were very important because they were inserted into metal brackets which became stock items when the cars were made and the selling and changing of the signs was done

by advertising agencies, many of which specialized in trolley advertising.

Young boys, hired by the ad agencies, usually handled the actual changing of the old signs and replacing them with new ones. One boy would stab the sign with a sharp, pointed stick, and lift it out with one motion. Another boy would follow and pick up the old signs. And still another would insert new signs into the brackets. With the demise of the trolley as a major form of transportation, signs similar to trolley car signs came into use on buses and subways.

For collectors, trolley car signs have always been one of the most desirable and sought after of all the signs used by The Coca-Cola Company to advertise their product. Unfortunately, early ones are very rare. Because of the type of material they were made of and their exposure to the heat and the cold, many of the trolley car signs, rare and otherwise, are found in rough condition. Many of the signs are found discolored which was caused by smoke from smoking passengers.

On the following pages you will find the largest number of trolley signs ever shown in one book, many of which are quite rare, as my estimated values will show. Keep in mind, however, that even though a large number of signs are shown in this book, it's just a sampling of the many used by The Coca-Cola Company over the years.

My personal favorites are signs which are representative of other advertising used for that particular year. In the years 1910, 1911, 1912, and 1913, for example, the artist Hamilton King's artwork was used on trays, calendars, magazine ads, and trolley car signs. Those are rare and very desirable. Finding signs which go along with the theme of other advertising of that year is always exciting and many do exist. Other signs have been found with artwork that was not used on any other advertising. In any case, they are all interesting and are very sought after by collectors.

c.1907 "Relieves Fatigue" $850.00

1912 "Hamilton King Art" . . . . . Rare $1,600.00

1914 . . . . $1,600.00

c.1912 . . . . $1,200.00

1923 "FLAPPER GIRL" $1,000.00

1923 "THE FOUR SEASONS" $850.00

1910 Featuring "The Coca-Cola Girl" by Hamilton King
and printed by Wolf & Co., Phila., Pa. $2,000.00

1914 "Two Girls" $1,500.00

1918 World War I Sugar Rationing Facts $500.00

c.1907 . . . . . . $800.00

c.1909 . . . . . $1,000.00

1927 ART BY FRED MIZEN $600.00

c.1908 . . . . $850.00

c.1914 . . . . $1,250.00

c.1914 . . . . $950.00

c.1918 . . . . $500.00

c.1914 . . . . $450.00

c.1913 . . . . $1,000.00

c.1918 . . . . $400.00

1922 (SUMMER) $2,500.00

1927 (FALL) 3 PIECE "LEAF" $1,000.00

c.1912 "SODA FOUNTAIN" 30"X 46"
CARDBOARD CUTOUT WINDOW DISPLAY
$4,000.00

1910 "MAN IN THE GRASS" (with glass)
28½"X 39½"
Printed by American Lithography
$2,000.00

(this cutout also exists in a bottle version)

c.1914 "COUPLE AT THE BEACH"
30"X 35"
$2,500.00

CHERUBS

NOTE: There is also a larger version of this Cherub probably used as a window display piece. The larger version is quite rare and worth considerably more than these smaller examples.

1908 "CHERUB" $1,600.00

Cardboard Cutout, Stand up (easel back) 14¾"

(Stand up Cherubs are Rare)

NOTE: The art work for the Cherub was copyright 1907, and probably not used until the following year 1908.

1908 "CHERUB" $1,500.00

Cardboard Cutout, Hanging (hole at top) 14¾"

CARDBOARD DISPLAY PIECES

1906 "Juanita" Cardboard Easel back
(Embossed Center) with Gold Trim 19"X26" $3,000.00

1930 18"X42" $450.00

1931 19"X27" Rockwell Art
Cardboard Cutout $750.00

1935 Rockwell Art 18"X36"
Printed by Snyder & Black $800.00

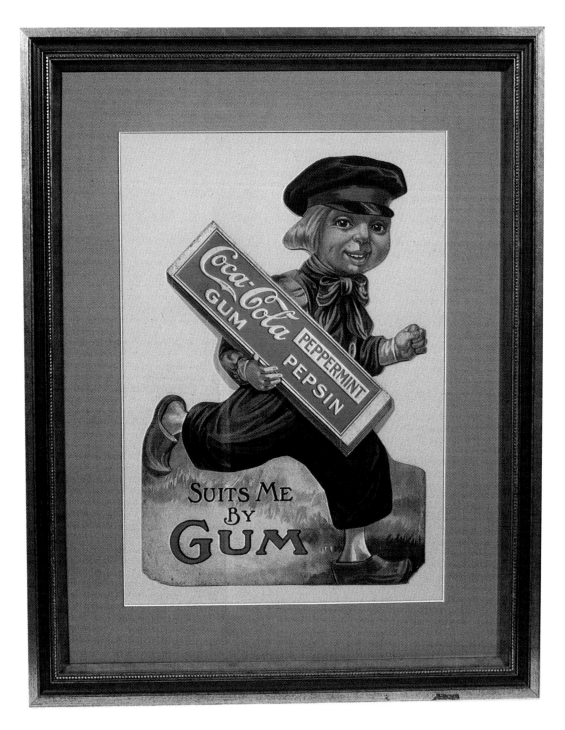

c.1914 - 1916 "Dutch Boy" Chewing Gum Cardboard Cutout
14"X 20½" . . . . Very Rare $3,000.00

c.1907 "ROSES" FESTOON
PRINTED BY WOLF & CO., PHILA.
$2,000.00

c.1909 FOLDOUT WINDOW DISPLAY
5' X 6'
VERY RARE WHEN FOUND COMPLETE
$5,000.00

1932 (MOVIE STAR) CARDBOARD CUTOUTS

Sue Carol $650.00

Lupe Velez $750.00

Frances Dee and Gene Raymond "At Malibu Beach"
25½"X 35½" $1,750.00

NOTE: Coca-Cola advertising featuring
movie stars are always desirable and
sought after by collectors. The more
famous the star, the more valuable the
piece. Jean Harlow is a perfect example.

Jean Harlow $1,500.00

Joan Blondell $850.00

CARDBOARD CUTOUTS

1931 10''X18½''
Easel back
Printed by Snyder & Black
$325.00

1924 36''X40'' Window Display . . $1,000.00

1938 15''X21½''
Hanging Sign
$175.00

1934 Window Display
Art by Haden Haden 31''X43'' $475.00

1939 32''X42''
Window Display Piece . . . $250.00

1897 ''VICTORIAN GIRL''
HEAVY CARDBOARD HANGING SIGN
6½'' X 10½''
VERY RARE $5,000.00

1905 ''LILLIAN NORDICA''
CELLULOID COVERED
CARDBOARD CAMEO SIGN
19''X 25''
RARE $4,000.00

CARDBOARD CUTOUTS

1902 8'' Hanging sign $2,000.00

1908 14¾'' ''Cherub'' $1,600.00

1926 ''Umbrella Girl'' (with bottle)
18''X 32'' $750.00

CARDBOARD CUTOUTS

1933 3-D Hanging Sign 10"X22"
Printed by Niagara Litho. $150.00

1933 3-D Hanging Sign 10"X22"
Printed by Niagara Litho. $150.00

1933 3-D Hanging Sign 10"X22"
Printed by Niagara Litho. $150.00

1924 11"X24"
Flower Box Window Display Piece . . . $125.00

1937 13"X34" Hanging Sign . . . $85.00

1924 "Flower Box"
15" X 20" . . $75.00

Late 30's "Swan" . . . $85.00

1924 "Flower Box"
15" X 20" . . $75.00

1932 10'' X 20'' 3-D
Printed by Niagara Litho., Co.
Buffalo, NY $200.00

1931 10'' X 20'' 3-D
Printed by Niagara Litho., Co.
Buffalo, NY $200.00

1933 10'' X 20'' 3-D
Printed by Niagara Litho., Co.
Buffalo, NY $200.00

1932 14'' $85.00

1950's 18'' $30.00

1930 10'' X 20'' 3-D Christmas Sign . . $200.00

CARDBOARD CUTOUTS

1930's 20" X 34" $150.00

1944 52" $175.00
(There is also a smaller version of this piece)

c.1938 22" X 23" $175.00

1953 13½" X 21" $50.00

1936 24¼" X 47¼" $275.00

1935 10¼" X 18½" . . . . $65.00 Each

-70-

CARDBOARD CUTOUTS

1944 "Service Girls" 25'' X 64'' . . . . . $175.00 Each   Complete set of 5 . . . . . $1,000.00

1944 "Service Girls" (Small size 17'')
$65.00 Each   Complete set of 5 . . . . $450.00

1926 "Specials Today" 15'' X 20''
$250.00

Refresh yourself my friend, and rest and feel you are a welcome guest.

DRINK Coca-Cola

1950 13'' X 22'' $45.00

DRINK Coca-Cola

See TV Here

TELEVISION

1950 24'' X 35'' $45.00

Drink Coca-Cola With good things to eat-

1939 30''X 42'' $175.00

COKE BELONGS

1948 . . . . . $35.00

Coca-Cola Coca-Cola

SO REFRESHING   SO DELICIOUS

1950's 16'' X 24'' . . . . $30.00 Each

CARDBOARD CUTOUTS

1944 19"X 15½" $100.00

1926 "Umbrella Girl" (with glass)
18"X 32" $750.00

NOTE: There is also a bottle version
of this cutout, shown on a color plate
in this book.

1949 27" X 31" . . . $165.00

1948 . . . $185.00

1927 23" X 30" $500.00

Early 1900's "Girl in Horseless Carrage"
Very Rare $3,000.00

CARDBOARD CUTOUTS

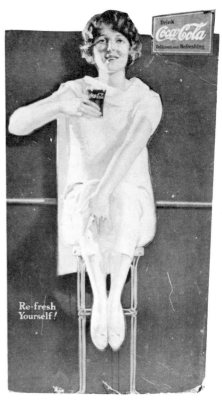

1920's 14''X 18'' printed by Niagara Litho Co., Buffalo, N.Y. . . . . . $350.00 Each

c.1926 16''X 29½'' $400.00

1952 21''X 30'' $60.00

1956 24''X 35'' $65.00

1952 20''X 28'' . . . $75.00

1960's 28''X 36'' $35.00

1956 3-D Easel back 15''X 18'' . . $125.00

1953 24''X 35'' $65.00

CARDBOARD CUTOUT BOTTLE DISPLAYS

1939 German . . . . $100.00 Pair

NOTE: Many collectors do shy away from foreign items, because of this even unusual pieces do not have the value of pieces produced for the U.S. market.

1926 "Girl Holding Tray"
11½"X 14" $225.00

1929 "Bathing Girl"
7"X 9¾" $250.00

Late 1920's "Boy and Weiner", 10"X 14" . . . $200.00

1930 "Girl in Swimsuit"
9"X 17½" $225.00

c.1933 (L.A. Bottling Co.) . . $125.00

1930's German 7" . . . $45.00

CARDBOARD CUTOUTS (SPRITE BOY)

1947 Display Signs . . . . $35.00 Each

1942 16''x 21'' (Snyder & Black) $185.00

1944 14''x 32'' $125.00

1960's 17''x 19'' (2 Sided) . . $100.00

1947 18''x 32'' $250.00

1941-48 14''x 25'' (Canadian) $125.00

1941-48 11'' (2 Sided) . . . $150.00

CARDBOARD CUTOUTS

1930's 8'' . . $65.00   1930's 9'' . . $45.00

1950's $15.00

1950's $15.00

1930's 7½''X 12'' $85.00

1960's $10.00

1949 . . . . $40.00

1920's 7½''X 12'' (2 sided) $285.00

1950's $25.00

1960's 10'' $15.00

1960's - 1970's ''Mobile'' $25.00

CARDBOARD CUTOUTS

Now! King size too!

You trust its Quality

Unmatched Sparkling Taste

SMART BIRDS GO FOR COKE

Coca-Cola

Enjoy that REFRESHING NEW FEELING

1960's "Mobile" "King Size" bottle display $35.00

1960's 36" "Penguin" $40.00

frozen Coca-Cola frozen frozen frozen

1960's vinyl $10.00

ICE COLD

1960's "Diamond Can" 8"X 10" . . $20.00

for EXTRA FUN...

take MORE HAN ON

c.1963 . . . . $50.00

1980's "Cabbage Patch Kids" cardboard cutouts . . . $15.00

FESTOONS

Festoons are cardboard cutout displays that were hung above the soda fountain backbar. During the 20's and 30's they were changed with the seasons. Found in original envelope would certainly increase it's value.

1922 . . . . . $1,500.00

1927 . . . . . $1,000.00

1951 . . . . . . $250.00

1958 . . . . . . $200.00

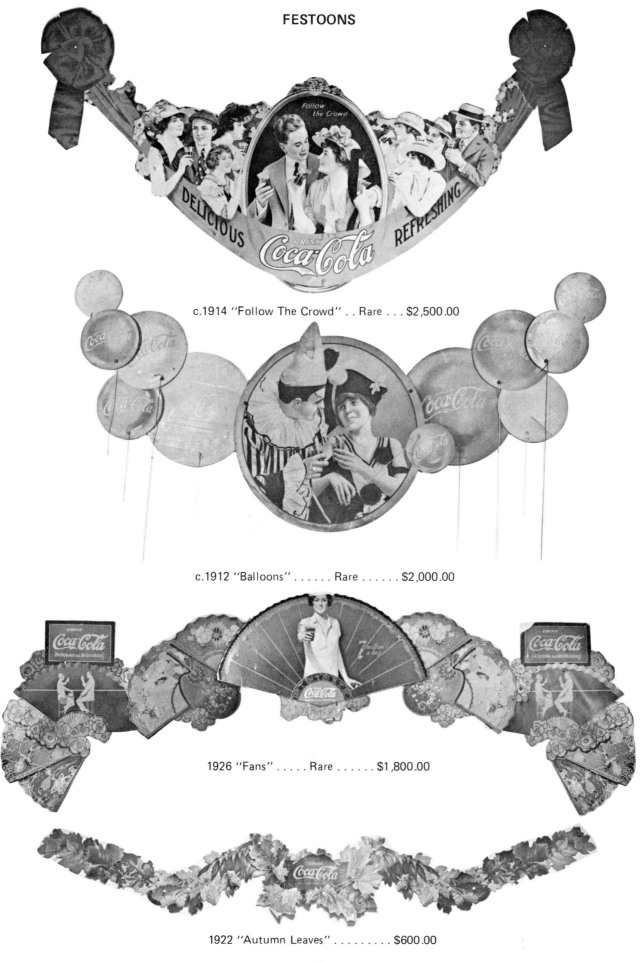

c.1914 "Follow The Crowd" . . Rare . . . $2,500.00

c.1912 "Balloons" . . . . . . Rare $2,000.00

1926 "Fans" . . . . . Rare $1,800.00

1922 "Autumn Leaves" $600.00

1932 FESTOONS

MORNING GLORY $500.00

HOLLYHOCK $500.00

CORNFLOWER $500.00

VERBENA $500.00

FESTOONS (BACKBAR DISPLAYS)

1930's "PETUNIA"
$325.00

1931 "POINSETTA" $500.00

1930's "LOCKET"
$350.00

1939 . . . . $225.00

NOTE: The prices on these Festoons and Backbar Displays are for complete examples. It's always nice to have the original envelope, and I'm sure it would enhance the value.

Late 30's "SWANS" $275.00

1950's "HOST TO THIRSTY MAIN STREET" $250.00

1950 . . . . $150.00

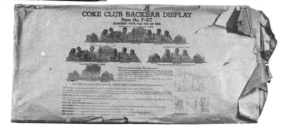

1950's "COKE CLUB" $275.00

FESTOONS (BACKBAR DISPLAYS)

-82-

1950's "STATE TREE" $185.00

1950's "SQUARE DANCE" $200.00

1951 "GIRLS HEADS" $225.00

1950's "ANTIQUE CARS" $200.00

1936 36"X 40" Cardboard cutout window display piece $250.00

1931 10"X 20" Cardboard cutout hanging sign $200.00

1932 Window display (5 pieces) $500.00

SANTAS
(cardboard display pieces)

1953 28"X 42" $50.00

1962 32"X 47" $75.00

1953 29"X 42" 3-D display . . $85.00

1949 15" easelback display
$85.00

1958 Cardboard display . . $18.00

1954 31"X 45" 3-D Display $85.00

SANTAS
(cardboard display pieces)

1950 9"X 14½" $65.00

1953 9"X 18½" 3D $50.00

1954 10½"X 19" $60.00

1953 9"X 18" $60.00

NOTE: These smaller size
Santa cutouts seem to be
more desirable and rarer
than the larger versions.

1948 7½"X 13½" $75.00

SANTAS

c.1952 11"X 22" paper banner . . . $20.00

1958 Hanger $10.00

1955 19" easelback display . . . $35.00

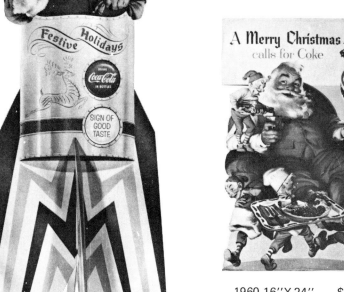

1957 13"X 33" 3-D Rocket Ship Display . . $125.00

1960 16"X 24" . . . $20.00

1970's 36" (English & French) . . . $6.00 Each

1960's Hanger $8.00

1958 Cardboard display . . . $18.00

SANTAS AND CHRISTMAS

1940's Window Display . $125.00

1959 Cutout
Hanger . . . $10.00

1958 Cutout
Hanger . . . $12.00

1946 6"X12"
Stand Up . . . $30.00

1970's 16"X24" . . . $8.00

1958 16"X27" . . . $15.00

1960's 16"X24" . . $10.00

1950's 36" . . $15.00

1964 16"X27" . . $10.00

1960's 36" Cutouts . . . . $10.00 Each

1953 12"X20"
Cutout . . . $25.00

1950's Carton Inserts
$4.00 Each

1953 14"X 18" . . $20.00

1959 Cutout
Hanger . . . $10.00

CARDBOARD SIGNS (MOVIE STARS)

1934 Wallace Beery
14"X30" $375.00

1934 Joan Crawford
14"X24"
$325.00

1934 Johnny Weissmuller and
Maureen O'Sullivan 14"X30"

$475.00

1935 Madge Evans 31"X41" Window Display
printed by Snyder & Black
$500.00

1932
Cardboard
Cutout
Display Pieces
13"X20½"

$250.00 Each

1934 Wallace Beery and Jackie Cooper
4½' Window Display $750.00

CARDBOARD SIGNS

1902 Hanging Sign 8" diameter
Photo shows both sides
Printed by Wolf & Co.
RARE $2,000.00

1914 "BETTY" 30"X 38" with wood frame . $1,000.00
This sign is rarely found in the original wood frame

1923 14"X 24" $750.00

CARDBOARD SIGNS

1924, 2 Poster Panoramic, (each poster 20''X 35½'') . . . . . $450.00 Each

1907 16''X 22'' Rare
as shown $1,600.00
complete $2,800.00

1931 21''X 38'' . . $375.00

1931 10''X 20'' . . . $375.00

(printed by Niagara Litho)

1937 14''X 30'' $200.00

1940's 16''X 27'' $150.00
(with wood frame)

1950's 16''X 27'' $85.00
(with wood frame)

1936 14''X 30'' $250.00

1943 16''X 27'' $150.00
(with wood frame)

c.1920's 8"X11" 3-D Hanging Sign . . $400.00

1934
14"X30"
$125.00

1935
Florine
McKinney
14"X30"
$225.00

1938 21"X44" . . $100.00

1938 14½"X32" . $100.00

1942 22" X 15" Self Framed Display, Printed by Snyder & Black
Cardboard display sign only . . . $75.00   Paper window banner only . . . $25.00
Complete set in envelope $125.00

Late 30's 14"X22" . . . $125.00

c.1920's Cardboard with Metal Frame
showing 2 1916 bottles 21"X60" . . $450.00

1937 22"X43"
Art by L. Wilbur
$175.00

1957 12"X14" . . . $35.00

CARDBOARD SIGNS

Home
refreshment
on the way

1945 16"X 27" $85.00

Refreshment right out of
the bottle

ICE COLD

1941 16"X 27" $85.00

"Talk about
refreshing"

DRINK
Coca-Cola

ICE COLD

1942 16"X 27" $85.00

Pause Refresh

Coca-Cola

You trust its quality

1950's 16"X 27" $35.00

Have a Coke

DRINK
Coca-Cola

c.1946 16"X 27" $50.00

DRINK Coca-Cola IN BOTTLES 5¢

1950's (Lillian Nordica) $175.00

Pause...refresh

DRINK
Coca-Cola

1950's 16"X 27" $60.00

SERVE
Coca-Cola
Sign of Good Taste

1958 20"X 36" $45.00

CARDBOARD SIGNS

1930's 9"X 12" $200.00

1953 16"X 27" $50.00

1950's 16"X 27" $35.00

1946 11"X 28" $50.00

1950's 16"X 16" $35.00

1946 20"X 36" "Outstanding Poster Award" . . $100.00

1940 14½"X 31½" . . . $100.00

1939 "The Girl on the Calendar - Through the Years"
27½"X 56" $350.00

1936 14"X 30" . . . $150.00

CARDBOARD SIGNS

1938 Sundblum Art 29''X50'' . . $350.00

1942 20'' X 36'' $100.00

1938 34''X50'' "Girl with Roses"
Inside Store Display $425.00

1929 19''X31'' . . $450.00

1950 16''X27'' $35.00

1942 16''X27'' $50.00

1941 29''X50'' . . . $100.00

NOTE: Remember Condition on these cardboard signs is very important. Fadding, creases and tears are common and certainly effect value.

1940 30''X50'' . . $125.00

1940's 30''X50'' . . .$100.00

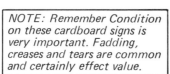

1937 32''X49'' . . $150.00

1960's 20''X36'' . . . $15.00

1930's 12''X18'' . . . $35.00

1960's 20''X36'' . . . $15.00

1960's 16''X27'' . . . $15.00

1950's 15''X18''
3-D Sign . . . $25.00

1950 22''X 45'' $75.00

1950's 16''X27'' . . . $35.00

1958 20''X36'' . . . $20.00

1938 12''X18'' $25.00

1958 16''X27'' . . . $25.00

1950's 20''X36'' . . $35.00

1940's 20''X36'' . . $85.00

1958 20''X36'' $45.00

CARDBOARD SIGNS

1941 20"X36" . . . $100.00

1956 20"X36" . . . $60.00

1955 16"X27" . . $30.00

1930's 12"X18" . . . $35.00

1953 22"X45" . . . $55.00

1946 16"X27" . . $40.00

1957 16"X27" . . . $30.00

1946 16"X27" . . . $50.00

1940's 27"X 56" . . $100.00

1940's 27"X 56" . . $100.00

CARDBOARD SIGNS

1935 10"X 15" Hanging Sign . . $100.00

1950's 20"X 36" . . . $45.00

1950's 18"X 24" Rand McNally Transcontinental
Mileage and Driving Time Chart $75.00

1942 20"X 36" $85.00

1948 16"X 27"
$40.00

1959 20"X 36"
$25.00

1960's 16"X 27"
$20.00

1940's 20"X 36"
$75.00

1950's 20"X 36" $25.00

1960's 20"X 36" $15.00

-97-

CARDBOARD SIGNS

1940's 20"X 36" with wood and metal insert frame $175.00

1950's 20"X 36" . . . $65.00

1940's 16"X 27" . $65.00

1950's 20"X 36" $45.00

1952 20"X 36" . . . $45.00

1940's 20"X 36" . . . $75.00

1942 20"X 36" . . . $100.00

1952 20"X 36" . . . $45.00

1946 20"X 36" . . . $75.00

1953 20"X 36" $45.00

CARDBOARD SIGNS

c.1930's 29"X50" . . . $300.00

1936 29"X50" . . . $300.00

1942 29"X50" . . . $150.00

c.1940's 29"X50" . $100.00

1941 29"X50" . . . $200.00

c.1940's 29"X50" . . $100.00

c.1940's 29"X50" . . $100.00

c.1940's 29"X50" . . $100.00

c.1940's 29"X56" $100.00

c.1940's 20"X36" . . $100.00

1953 20"X36" . . $100.00

1944 20"X36" . . . $85.00

1949 20"X36" . . . $60.00

CARDBOARD SIGNS

1950's 16"X 27" $45.00

1960's 16"X 27" . . $25.00

1960's 16"X 27" . . $20.00

1959 16"X 27" $35.00

1960's 20"X 36" $20.00

1969 14"X 14" . . . $15.00

1960's 16"X 27" . . . $25.00

1960's 20"X 36" $20.00

1960's 20"X 36" $20.00

1970's 16"X 27" $10.00

1950's 20"X 36" $25.00

1960's 19"X 27" $15.00

CARDBOARD SIGNS

1970's 16"X 26" . . . $10.00

1976 20"X 29" . . . $8.00

1960's 16"X 27" . . . $15.00

1959 16"X 26" . . . $25.00

1960's 20"X 38" with alu. frame $25.00

Let Us Deliver A CHRISTMAS CARTON OF Coca-Cola TO YOUR HOME 27¢ PROMPT SERVICE

1950's 14"X 24" . . . $20.00

1960's 20"X 38" with alu. frame $25.00

1979 21"X 39" $10.00

1970's Repro tray offer . . . $10.00

1959 16"X 26" . . . $25.00

ALL TIME SPORTS FAVORITE
(CARDBOARD SIGNS)

1947 "ALL TIME SPORTS FAVORITE" Hanging Cardboard Signs.
13"X 15" printed by Snyder & Black, the complete set consists of
10 signs: Ty Cobb, Willie Hoppe, Red Grange, Man O' War, Gene
Tunney, Ned Day, Colonial Lady M, Bobby Jones, Helene Madison,
Don Budge.

Individule Signs . . . . $40.00 Each
Complete Set of 10 . . . .$450.00

NOTE: I have seen individual "All Time Sports Favorite" signs sell for higher
than my estimated value of $40.00 each. To a baseball collector for example
the Ty Cobb sign may be worth more to him. Also if a particular sign is
needed to complete a set.

BASEBALL PLAYERS (CARDBOARD SIGNS)

1950's PHIL RIZZUTO
10"X 12" $175.00

ROY CAMPANELLA
12"X 17½" $175.00

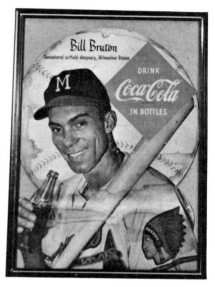

BILL BRUTON
11"X 14" $175.00

MONTE IRVIN
11"X 14" $175.00

LARRY DOBY
11"X 14" $175.00

SATCHEL PAIGE
11"X 14" $175.00

1950'S CELEBRITY ADVERTISING

NOTE: Movie, sports stars and celebrity advertising pieces are always very popular among collectors.

Kit Carson, Apache & El Toro in the "Adventures of Kit Carson"

LIONEL HAMPTON
11"X14" $150.00

SUGAR RAY ROBINSON
11"X14" ... $175.00

1953 Mailer Card for
Kit Carson
Kerchief $15.00

1955 Kit Carson
"Rodeo Tie" . . $50.00

1953 KIT CARSON PAPER SIGN
16"X24" $25.00

1953
KIT CARSON
KERCHIEF
20"X 22" $35.00

1951 MARIO LANZA PAPER WINDOW BANNER
11"X22" $35.00

1953 KIT CARSON
PAPER WINDOW BANNER
16"X24" $35.00

AIRPLANE HANGERS
(CARDBOARD SIGNS)

1941 20" X 22" WITH STRING HANGERS . . . . . . $30.00 Each

1943 13" X 15" WITH STRING HANGERS . . . . . $20.00 Each
COMPLETE SET OF 20 HANGERS WITH ORIGINAL ENVELOPE $450.00

BANNERS, UMBRELLAS, FLAGS

c.1911 Canvas Banner 16"X 11' $1,500.00

c.1914 Canvas Banner 16"X 72" $1,000.00

c.1910 Canvas Banner 9"X 48" $1,500.00

NOTE: Banners showing the straight side bottle are more desirable than without.

c.1911 Canvas Banner 9"X 48" $1,000.00

1920's
Umbrella
$750.00

NOTE:
Earlier Umbrellas showing the straight side bottle would certainly be worth more. $1,000.00 - $1,250.00

c.1936 Truck Flag $50.00

1950's Canvas Truck Banner 48"X 64" $275.00

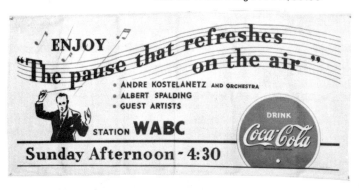

c.1939 Canvas Truck Banner 24"X 50" $350.00

c.1950 Canvas Truck Banner 64"X 44" . . . $225.00

1950 Cloth Banner 18½"X 56" $200.00

SELF FRAMED TIN SIGNS

1907 "Relieves Fatigue"
18½"X27" $4,000.00

1905 Lillian Nordica
23"X 33" . . . . . $1,600.00 (as shown)
Excellent to Near Mint condition . . . $4,500.00

1914 "Betty" 31"X 41" $2,000.00

1916 20"X 30½" $1,500.00

STRAIGHT SIDED BOTTLE SIGNS

The straight sided Coca-Cola bottle signs are certainly the most sought after Coca-Cola signs. The values you see here are for signs in nice clean presentable condition, signs in poor or less than excellent condition would be priced considerably less. Signs in Mint condition could be worth more.

1910-1914 18" X 30" Cardboard $750.00

1910-1914 19" X 27" Tin $600.00

NOTE: It's very common to find these early signs in poor condition. Keep in mind that every scratch, dent, and pitted area does effect the value.

1970's 19" X 27" Tin . . . $100.00
Reproduction

NOTE: "Trade Mark Registered" appears under the logo on the repro and in the tail of the "C" on the original.

c.1908 12" X 36" Tin $650.00

c.1908 12" X 36" Tin $600.00

TIN AND CELLULOID SIGNS

1927 8½"X11" TIN $700.00

1926 8½"X11" TIN $700.00

1927 8½"X 11" TIN $350.00

1926 TIN OVAL . . . $1,250.00

1927 Embossed Tin 20"X 15" . . $1,400.00

1921 6"X11¼" CELLULOID $550.00
Black with Gold trim manufactured by Whitehead
& Hoag Co., Newark, N.J.

1929 Embossed Tin 20"X 15" $850.00

1922 6"X 13¼" Tin $350.00

1920's Embossed Tin 20"X 15" $850.00

GLASS SIGNS

1950 Glass and plastic (hanging sign) $300.00

1950's Glass and plastic (counter sign) $200.00

c.1940's Decal and etched glass $175.00

1932 10"X 22" $800.00

1932 6"X 12" $750.00

1930's 6"X 9½" . . $175.00

1932 12" oval $850.00

1932 12"X 20" $1,500.00
Manufactured by "The Brunhoff Mfg. Co."
Display Advertising Specialists.

1932 24" stand up "Fan" sign . . . $1,000.00

1932 24" hanging "Fan" sign . . . $1,000.00

c.1950's 11'' "CASH REGISTER TOPPER" . $100.00
Glass on wood base, enameled "Coke" plate on wood.

Late 1930's 10¼'' X 14¼''
Metal framed $175.00

c.1930's 2 Bottle Mirror
3''X 7'' $85.00

1950's Glass with wood base . . $200.00

c.1939 10¼''X 14¼''
with thermometer . . . $200.00

Early 1920's to Mid 1930's, 11¼'' Dia.
Reverse on glass, mirror sign . . . $250.00

c.1930's 10''X 14¼''
Metal framed $200.00

Late 1920's
8''X 17¾'' . . $250.00

c.1930's 8¼''X 18¼''
Metal framed $200.00

1937 10''X 12'' Glass Sign $450.00
Reverse on glass, foil back, metal frame.

c.1940 5''X 15'' Reverse Glass . . . $325.00

ARROW SIGNS

1939-41
Masonite and Aluminum $175.00

Late 1930's Wood and Aluminum . . . $150.00

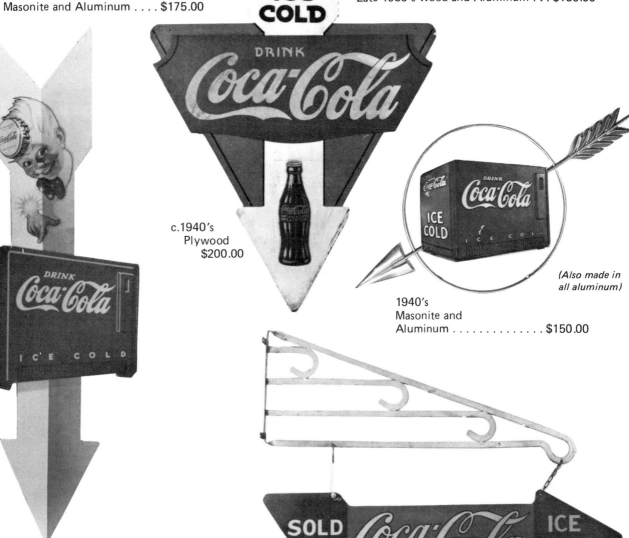

c.1940's
Plywood
$200.00

1940's
Masonite and
Aluminum $150.00

(Also made in
all aluminum)

1940's Masonite 30'' . . . $175.00

1927 - 1929 7¾''X 30'' Tin (2 sided)
Sign only $350.00
with original metal hanging bracket $500.00
NOTE: I have seen two different types of these arrow signs.
I have also seen them dated both 1927 and 1929.

PORCELAIN SIGNS

NOTE: *Porcelain signs very often have scrapes or rub marks, this should be considered when determining value.*

Late 1930's 22''X 26'' . . . $350.00

Late 1930's
24''X26'' $375.00

c. 1950's 28''X28'' . . . $225.00

1934 14''X27'' $300.00

c. 1930's 10''X28'' . . . $200.00

c. 1950's 12''X28'' $100.00

c. 1950's 12''X28'' . . $125.00

LATE 30's 14''X27'' . . .$275.00

(Also made in masonite)

c. 1950's 12''X28'' $100.00

c. 1950's 16''X24''

$85.00

-113-

PORCELAIN SIGNS

1960's 28"X 28" . . $85.00

1950's 28"X 32" . . $175.00

1940's 12"X 29" $225.00

Late 1930's 4'X 5'   (Tenn. Enamel Mfg. Co.) $450.00

1950's 24"X 24" $85.00

1940's Canadian (French) 36" . . . $100.00

1930's 18"X 24" $125.00

1950's 12"X 28" $100.00

-114-

TIN CUTOUT SIGNS

1950's 16''
Tin $45.00
Porcelain . . $60.00

1951 11''X 12'' . . $125.00

1959 11''X 12'' . . $75.00

1933-34 3' Embossed . . . $300.00

Early 1950's
3' Embossed . . $275.00

1950's 3' Flat $250.00

1963 30''X 36'' . . . $125.00

c.1955 13''X 20'' . . . $125.00

1960's 30''X 35'' . . $125.00

FLANGE SIGNS

NOTE: A flange sign is a sign with a metal flange at a right angle to the sign, allowing it to be attached to the side of a building and be seen from both sides.

ENJOY Coca-Cola IN BOTTLES

c.1948 "Enjoy" Rare $225.00

1938 Canadian (French)
18"X 20" $125.00

c.1948 . . . . . $125.00

1950's $85.00

1934 . . . . $150.00

1930's 12"X 16" $200.00

ICED Coca-Cola HERE

1949 Canadian
Porcelain $250.00

1960 (2 different examples) . . $45.00 Each

1950's $100.00

1940's $125.00

TIN SIGNS

1922 4''X 8''
2 different examples . . . . $225.00 Each

1931
18''X 54'' . . $350.00

1930's ''Gas Today'' 20''X 28''
Rare $400.00

1920's 12''X 36'' $350.00

1930
20''X 15'' $300.00

1934 20'' $200.00

1927 28''X 29'' Rare $450.00

c.1910 24''X 58'' Cross Press & Sign Co., Chicago. $400.00

TIN SIGNS

1938 18"X 54" $225.00

1930 20"X 27" $275.00

1936 12"X 36" $175.00

1936 10"X 28" $200.00

1931 9"X 12" $185.00

1948 16"X 32" $175.00

1936 12"X 36" $200.00

1940's 12"X 36" $175.00

1930's 20"X 28" $275.00

1930's 19"X 54" $200.00

1940's 20"X 28" . . $200.00
(Also made in masonite. Beware
of masonite reproduction.)

1920's 12"X 17" wood base . . $100.00
(This is a top sign for an Icy-O cooler, rev.
has instructions on how to use the cooler.)

c.1936 19"X 54" $375.00

1940's 19"X 54" $175.00

TIN SIGNS

1934 19''X 28''
Green background $325.00

1950's 12''X 25'' $65.00

1950's 10''X 28'' . . . $65.00

1937 19''X 28'' . . . $125.00

1934 19''X 28''
White background $285.00

1934 . . . . $325.00

1934 45½'' $350.00

1940 19''X 54'' . $175.00

1930's 19''X 54'' . $250.00

1948
16''X 40'' . $85.00

$275.00 $175.00
1930's 19''X 54'' (2 different examples)

1930's 19''X 54''
$250.00

Coca-Cola
Sold Here
Ice Cold

1920's 19''X 54''
$350.00

TIN SIGNS

DRINK Coca-Cola

1941   11"X 35" $175.00

1941   11"X 35" $175.00

1941 19"X 54" . $225.00

1941 20"X 28" $250.00

1941 20"X 28" $250.00

1941 19"X 54" . $225.00

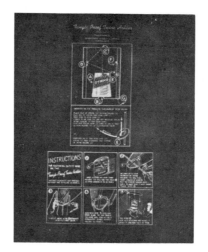

1930's String Holders 14"X 16" showing 2 different examples, plus (reverse side) instructions . . . . $285.00 Each

1930's 19"X 28" . . $125.00

1950's 19"X 28"
$85.00

1930's 19"X 54"
$175.00

1950 18"X 54"
$150.00

1948 16"X 40" . . $65.00

1930's 19"X 54" . . $175.00

TIN SIGNS

1930's 5¾''X 17¾'' (Dasco) $75.00

1922 6''X 23'' $100.00

1926 10½''X 31'' $185.00

1939
19''X 28'' . $100.00

1934
19''X 28'' . $175.00

1934
19''X 28'' . . $150.00

1950's 10''X 24'' $30.00

1950's - 60's Menu Board 14''X 53'' $100.00

1960's
Calendar Holder . . $40.00

1960's
Tire Rack Sign . . $60.00

1950's 10''X 24'' . . $30.00

1940's 16''X 36''
Canada $75.00

1950's 36''X 36'' $65.00

1963 20''X 28'' . . . $45.00

1964 20''X 28'' . . . $60.00

1964 20''X 28'' $50.00

1948 19''X 28'' . . . $60.00

1950 19''X 28'' . . $65.00

1964 19''X 28'' . $50.00

1960's 11''X 28'' . . . $30.00

1950's Sprite Boy
Rack Sign $50.00

1950's 19''X 28'' . . $50.00

1964 24''X 24'' . . $45.00

1963
18''X 54'' . . $60.00

1950's 20''X 28'' $50.00

1964 11''X 28'' $50.00

1963 11''X 28'' $45.00

1980's 24''X 24'' . . . . $10.00 Each

ENJOY 12oz. KING SIZE

Coca-Cola

ICE COLD HERE

ENJOY BIG KING SIZE

Coca-Cola

ICE COLD HERE

20''X28'' ''King Size'' 2 different
versions . . . . $45.00 Each

Coca-Cola
SIGN OF GOOD TASTE
Take home a carton
BIG KING SIZE

20''X28'' $50.00

Coca-Cola
SIGN OF GOOD TASTE

11''X28'' $45.00

ICE COLD
Coca-Cola
SIGN OF GOOD TASTE

20''X28'' $45.00

Coca-Cola

11''X28'' $60.00

DRINK
Coca-Cola
Coke Refreshes You Best!
SEPTEMBER 1963
10 TUESDAY

1963 Calendar
Sign $50.00

Coca-Cola
SIGN OF GOOD TASTE
BIG KING SIZE
ICE COLD

Coca-Cola
SIGN OF GOOD TASTE
ICE COLD

ICE COLD
DRINK
Coca-Cola
SIGN OF GOOD TASTE
PREPARED BY THE BOTTLER OF COCA-COLA

20''X28'' 3 different versions . . . . $45.00 Each

Coca-Cola
SIGN OF GOOD TASTE
ICE COLD

DRINK Coca-Cola ENJOY THAT Refreshing NEW FEELING ICE COLD

18''X 54'' $60.00

18''X 54'' $60.00

1950's DISC (BUTTON) SIGNS

24" With Bottle . . $175.00

24" Bottle Only . $150.00

36" Bottle Only . . .$150.00

36" . . . $65.00

36" With Bottle . . . $175.00

DRINK Coca-Cola

36" . . . $60.00

36" . . . $65.00

18" $125.00

DRINK Coca-Cola IN BOTTLES

24" . . . $50.00

24" . . . $50.00

12" . . . $35.00

12" . . . $35.00

18" . . . $40.00

MENU BOARDS

1939
WOOD AND MASONITE
$175.00

1939
WOOD AND MASONITE
$150.00

LATE 50's WOOD $50.00

1934 TIN $75.00

1939 TIN $75.00

c.1960 TIN $35.00

c.1960's TIN $35.00

c.1950's TIN $30.00

1970's TIN $15.00

MENU BOARDS

1940's Wood with Metal Trim $150.00

Reverse Glass
Metal Frame . . $75.00

1950's Cardboard . . $40.00

Late 40's
Cardboard . . $50.00

1950's Cardboard . . $45.00

1950's Plastic . . $25.00

c.1960 . . . $30.00

1960's . . $30.00

1960's Plastic
with clock . . $75.00

1950's
Cardboard . . $40.00

1950's Porcelain . . $75.00
(Canada)

1960's . . . $35.00

1950's . . . $45.00

1970's Tin . . $10.00

1929 Tin . . $125.00

MENU BOARDS

Late 1930's wood $175.00

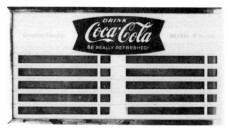

1960's Plastic and metal $85.00

1970's Plastic . . . $15.00

1960's Plastic $60.00

c.1964 . . . . $35.00

1960's $35.00

1950's Porcelain . . . $60.00
(Canada)

1970's Plastic . . . $8.00

Plastic & Cork
Message Center . . $8.00

1940's French . . $30.00 1940's English . . $50.00
(Canada)

MISCELLANEOUS SIGNS

1940's 8"X 14" "Lunch"
(wood cutout) $100.00

Late 1930's 11"X 39" Kay Displays (wood cutout) $175.00

Late 1930's 20"X 39" wood menu board $200.00

Late 1930's
19"X 20"
wood with metal trim $250.00

c.1940's 11"X 39"
wood and masonite
with gold trim . . $175.00

1940's 12"X 16½" wood and metal . . $100.00

Late 1930's
19"X 19"
wood with metal trim . . . Rare . . . $375.00

1940's 12" wood $65.00

1940's 13" fiberboard . . . $100.00

-128-

1940's Masonite and Wood signs . . . . $45.00 Each   Complete set $350.00

1930's Wood with Metal brackets
delivery truck roof sign $350.00

NOTE: During the late 1930's and 1940's masonite and wood were used on many signs to advertise Coca-Cola. Kay Displays was one of the major manufacturers of these specialty signs. You will find their name stamped on the back of many wood, masonite, and fiberboard signs of this period.

1950's - 1960's Wood and Metal (2 sided) . . . $65.00

Late 1930's 36'' Wood $375.00

1941 Wood and Masonite 14''X 36'' . . . $175.00

1960's 7''X 16'' Masonite and Plastic with rope . . $45.00

Late 1930's tin and wood $125.00

Late 1930's
8'' tin (with ribbon)
hanging sign $85.00

1930's 5¾''X 17¾'' tin embossed
(2 different examples) . . $50.00 Each

1931 tin embossed
6''X 13½'' . $175.00

1931 tin embossed
4½''X 12½'' . $150.00

1970's License Plates (3 different examples) . . . $10.00 Each

1922 4''X 8'' tin embossed
(2 different examples) . . $225.00 Each

WILL RETURN AT

1950's 6''X 6'' . . $40.00

1950's - 1960's
Parking Meter sign . . $65.00

1940's - 1950's
plastic and metal
''Bottle Shaped''
''Door Pull'' . . $65.00

Late 1930's ''Bottle Shaped''
aluminium, ''Door Pull'' . . $125.00

1960's 4''X 6''
''Pull Plate'' . . $30.00

1940's - 1950's
''Pull Plate'' . . $50.00

DOOR PUSH BARS

1930's Porcelain (complete with wrought iron end pieces) . . . . $275.00   Porcelain center piece only $175.00

1939-41 . . . . $125.00

c.1960 Porcelain $85.00

1950's Porcelain $100.00

1950's Porcelain $125.00

1950's Porcelain $75.00

1950's - 60's (Adjustable) $45.00

1950's Porcelain (French) Canada $50.00

1970's - 80's (French) Canada $20.00

PLASTIC SIGNS

1960's 3-D cutout "Race Cars" . . . . . $25.00 Each   Complete set of 4 . . . . $125.00

1950 12"X 14" . . . $25.00

1960's 3-D . . . $10.00

1960's 3-D $10.00

1950's - 60's 5'7'' plastic with raised letters and aluminum ring
$175.00

1960's 10"X 18" . . . $10.00

1960's 9"X 32" "Pop Corn" $30.00

1970's 3-D $5.00

1960's 3-D cutout . . . . $10.00 Each

1960's 14"X 20" $10.00

SMALL SIGNS

1932 Floral Boxes (pressed paper and cardboard)
Small Size . . . . $185.00 Each   Large Size $250.00

BOTTLERS

c.1950's 9" Celluloid Sign
Mint in original instruction envelope $85.00

NOTE: The bottle version of these signs is certainly the best looking, but also the most common.

c.1950's (sign only) . . . $40.00

9" Celluloid Signs from the late 1930's to the 1950's
(5 different examples shown)

c.1940's $50.00

DRINK
Coca-Cola
"Coke"
WE LET YOU SEE THE BOTTLE

c.1940's $60.00

1950's Plastic "Bottle Topper" . . . $75.00

NOTE: The two small gold bottles on this piece are original and must be attached to be complete.

PAUSE
DRINK Coca-Cola
GO REFRESHED

c.1950's $65.00

Drink
Coca-Cola
Delicious and Refreshing

1938 . . . . . $75.00

-133-

LIGHT UP SIGNS

1948 12"X 20" $375.00

1948 12"X 20"
Hanging Sign $500.00

1948 12"X 20" $375.00

With Clock ... $225.00

1948 12"X 20" .. $375.00

1950's
LIGHT UP COUNTER SIGNS
9"X 20"

Waterfalls (Motion) ... $375.00

Square Clock ... $225.00

Waterfalls (Motion) ... $375.00

With Clock $225.00

With Clock ... $225.00

With Clock ... $225.00

Pause (Motion) $375.00

With Clock ... $225.00

With Clock ... $225.00

With Clock ... $225.00

Late 1930's Reverse Glass, 12''X 14'' ''The Brunhoff Mfg. Co., Display Advertising Specialties, Cinci., Ohio'' $1,200.00

Late 1920's Reverse Glass, 7''X 15''X 5'' deep, ''The Cincinnati Advertising Products Company'' . . . Rare $750.00

1939-1941 Reverse Glass, light up, (motion) sign . . . $500.00

1959 Light up counter sign, chrome 16'' high $375.00
(There is also a counter dispenser that matched this light up sign)

1960's Glass front, metal frame, 8''X 14'' . . $45.00

1950's Glass front, metal frame, 8''X 18'' $125.00

1956 Plastic 28''X 36'' hanging signs
2 different versions . . . . $100.00 Each

(1)

c.1936 12"X 23" Hanging Neon Sign . . $1,600.00
(Transformer marked: "Property The Coca-Cola Co.,
342 Madison Ave., NYC")

c.1930's 12"X 20"
Light-up "Moving" Sign
3 photo's shown:

1. "Drink Coca-Cola"
2. Changing
3. "The pause that Refreshes"

Wood box with cardboard slats that
move and change messages. A very
unusual and rare piece that very
possibly could be a prototype and
even a "One of a kind" $2,500.00

(2)

(3)

1930's "Drug Store" Neon Sign 15"X 24"
chrome (boxed in) art deco . . . Rare $2,000.00
(Mfg. Electron Signs, Inc., Chicago, Ill.)

LIGHT UP SIGNS

Late 1940's 18"X 28" Neon Sign . . $1,000.00

1920's - 1930's Milk Glass Globe
(with hardware) $600.00
NOTE: I have seen a few different styles of these
globes, they all seem to have about the same value.

1960's 5"X18" $20.00

1950's 8"X 18" Glass front . . .$125.00

PAUSE DRINK Coca-Cola REFRESH

1950's 10"X 17" Plastic front $150.00

Refresh Yourself DRINK Coca-Cola

1950's 10"X17"
Plastic front $150.00

Have a Coke DRINK Coca-Cola Refresh Yourself

1950 10"X 17" Plastic front $125.00

PLEASE PAY WHEN SERVED DRINK Coca-Cola

1950's 8"X 18" Glass front $125.00

DRINK Coca-Cola IN BOTTLES

1960's 8"
Plastic front $125.00

NO EXTRA CHARGE FOR DRINK Coca-Cola TOAST OR GRILL

1950's 28"X 36" Plastic front,
hanging sign $100.00

Coca-Cola SIGN OF GOOD TASTE

1960's 8"X 18" Plastic front . . . $50.00

ENJOY Coca-Cola

1960's 5"X14"
Plastic front $30.00

DRINK Coca-Cola SIGN OF GOOD TASTE

1965 12"
Glass front $35.00

LIGHT UP SIGNS

1960's Plastic, 2 sided hanging sign $100.00

1950's Plastic, (metal base) stand up sign $225.00

1950's 17"X 17" Plastic, with cardboard inserts $125.00

1950's 17"X 17" Plastic, with cardboard inserts $125.00

1960's Plastic, 2 sided hanging sign $100.00

1960's 18"X 18" Plastic $50.00

1960's 12"X 17" Plastic front . . . $65.00

1960's 14"X 32" Plastic front $50.00

COLD DRINKS

1970's Glass front, counter sign 3"X 20" . . . $20.00

1950's "Wall Basket" metal, light up $40.00

ENJOY Coca-Cola

1960's 12"X 38" Plastic front $50.00

1960's Plastic and Tin, Lantern signs . . . . . $45.00 Each

THERMOMETERS

1915 WOOD 5"X21"
$275.00

1905 WOOD
4"X15"
$285.00

1944 MASONITE
7"X 17" . . $100.00

1941 TIN 7"X16"
$100.00

1939 TIN 6½"X16"
$85.00

1936 TIN 7"X16"
$85.00

c.1950's 9"
$45.00

1939 2 different examples . . $100.00 Each
(Canada)

1929
$150.00
(Canada)

1930's TIN 17"
$100.00

1950's TIN 17"
$40.00

1958 TIN 17"
$25.00

c.1948 9"
$35.00

1956 Gold Bottle
2¼"X7½" $10.00

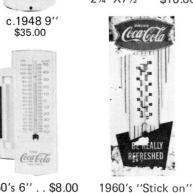

1960's 6" . . $8.00

1960's "Stick on"
7" $10.00

c.1948 32"
Rare . . $450.00

-139-

1950's Tin 30" . . . . $65.00 Each
(2 different examples)

1958 TIN 30" $65.00

THERMOMETERS AND PUSH PLATES

Early 1900's
5"X 21" $300.00

1929 French . . $100.00
(Canada)

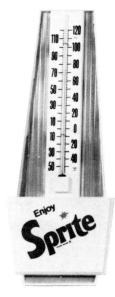

1960's Plastic . . $25.00

1960's Sprite
Plastic . . $10.00

c.1905 Aluminum Push/Pull Plates
Mfg. N.J. Aluminum Co., Newark, N.J.

Push Plate 3"X 8" $225.00
Pull Plate 2¼"X 8" $225.00

$85.00

$40.00

1930's
PORCELAIN
PUSH
PLATES

(Canada)

$45.00

$85.00

$40.00

THERMOMETERS
ROUND/GLASS FRONT

NOTE: Prices on these thermometers are based on working examples with glass. Thermometers found without front glass would be worth considerably less.

Early 50's
12" $150.00

1964
18¼" . . . $85.00

1959
12" . . . $100.00

1964
12" . . . $65.00

1970's
12" . . . $25.00

1960's
18¼" . . . $75.00

1950's
12" . . . $60.00

1957
12" . . . $60.00

1960's
12" . . . $60.00

1950's
12" . . . $60.00

CLOCKS

In the early days of Coca-Cola, the clock was certainly not considered an important advertising tool. Because of the cost it would be impractical to justify its use in advertising Coca-Cola. This would soon change, and in the mid-1890's, The Coca-Cola Company would not only use the clock to advertise but, it would also realize that it was a long lasting effective item that would more than justify the initial expense.

Because no evidence has proven otherwise, we do assume that the Baird Clock was the first to advertise the product. Edward Payson Baird was born in Philadelphia, Pennsylvania on January 26, 1860. As a young man, he worked for the William Torrey Co. The Torrey Co. made boxes for the Seth Thomas Clock Co., Baird became fascinated by the clock making business and in 1888, he started the Edward P. Baird and Co., Clock Manufacturers in Montreal, Canada. In 1890, he moved his company to Plattsburg, N.Y. It is here that he began to manufacture Coca-Cola advertising clocks. Baird is known to clock collectors mainly for his cases. He never made the movements for his clocks. In fact, his clocks were advertised as containing Seth Thomas movements. I have seen movements stamped "Seth Thomas" and "Baird Clock Co." Even movements stamped "Baird" were made by other clock makers, probably, Seth Thomas. Baird's main contribution to clock making was the use of papier-mache in mass produced advertising clocks. They were produced easily and quickly at a low cost and because of this he was a leader in the field.

From 1893 to 1896, Baird produced many different versions of the wood case and papier-mache (advertising portion) Coca-Cola clocks, most of which you will see on the following pages. Keep in mind that the advertising portion of these clocks (top and bottom rings) are made of molded papier-mache, which is sometimes mistaken for wood, and can't be cleaned with solvent or any other solution. Solvent will dissolve the papier-mache and within minutes, you will own a completely worthless clock. During this "Plattsburg era", Baird produced two types of clocks for Coca-Cola, the "figure eight" and "gallery", both papier-mache. It seems that with every order for clocks, The Coca-Cola Company had the style and advertising message changed. It also seems that the molds for the papier-mache didn't last very long, which accounts for the many different styles that have turned up over the years. The early "medicinal" claims predated some of the more toned down "delicious and refreshing" versions.

In 1896, Baird moved his plant again, this time to Chicago, and with this move he changed his clocks completely. The "Chicago era" Baird clocks were now a wood case with tin embossed advertising and dial portion on top and a tin embossed bottom door outlined with wood. I, personally, believe that the Coca-Cola Chicago clock was made in 1899 or 1900. This clock has been shown in an earlier Coca-Cola price guide erroneously dated 1892. I also believe that this clock was made for a very short period of time and in very limited numbers which would account for the fact that very few of these "Chicago era" clocks have turned up over the years. In later years, Baird became famous for his inventions relating to telephone toll apparatus, locks and keys, but he will always be best known to Coca-Cola collectors, as the manufacturer of the first clock to advertise the product.

In 1901, The Coca-Cola Co. used the Welch clock to advertise their product. The E.N. Welch Mfg. Co., of Forestville, Ct., produced a well made dependable clock which I happen to think is the most beautiful and desirable Coca-Cola clock. It was basically an octagon school house, regulator clock with a paper face printed with the Coca-Cola logo and a brass bezel and glass door. But what really makes this clock great was an advertising piece in the bottom door behind the pendulum. You will see two versions of this shown on the following pages.

Between the years 1903 and 1907, Ingraham clocks were used to advertise Coca-Cola. Both an octagon school house clock and a standard store regulator. These were both key wound, eight day movements and are more common than the Welch clocks. Beginning in 1910, the Wm. L. Gilbert Clock Co., Winsted, Ct., began producing clocks for Coca-Cola and were the most common store regulators used by the company. They were used almost exclusively between 1910 and 1940 when the use of the eight day regulator clock was discontinued.

The Gilbert clock was very dependable and well made, and seemed to run forever with very little care. These clocks all had "Coca-Cola" faces (Coca-Cola is printed in red.), but they are very often found faded. There are a number of different types of faces, but all had standard Arabic numerals. They also had gold painted, glass bottom doors. This gold painting was done by stencil which accounts for the fact that the lettering sometimes looked crude. Be very careful with these clocks, reproduction paper dials and new bottom glass is available and often put in old clocks and sold to the unsuspecting collector.

Prior to 1915, The Coca-Cola Co. also used a number of small clocks in the form of celluloid covered and gold stamped leather clocks, some of which, I have also shown in this section.

In the early 1930's, the company began using electric clocks and in the late 1930's and into the early 1940's, some of these clocks were the neon, light-up type, which are very popular among collectors and bring premium prices today.

After World War II, the use of the advertising clock really took off and the 1950's saw a large variety of clocks in metal and glass, aluminum, plastic, and neon and other light-up clocks. Of course, the illuminated types are always more desirable and they became very popular in the 1960's, both in glass and plastic. During the 1970's, The Coca-Cola Co. still used a wide variety of clocks both illuminated and not, most of which were made in plastic.

With all of the different types of clocks used by The Coca-Cola Co. over the years, it is no wonder why they have become a favorite item among collectors.

BAIRD CLOCKS

BAIRD "GALLERY" CLOCK
(2 different examples shown)
The "Gallery" clock is considered much rarer than the figure "8" versions.

c.1891 - 1895 (upper and lower case letters)
Time only $3,750.00

c.1891 - 1895 (upper case letters)
Time and Strike . . . Very Rare $5,000.00

c.1891 - 1895 Baird Clocks Figure "8" versions (Plattsburg Era) 3 different examples shown . . . $3,600.00

BAIRD (Chicago Era) CLOCK
(2 different examples shown)

c.1896 - 1900 (8 day movement)
bottom door not original $3,000.00

c.1896 - 1900 (15 day movement)
all original $5,000.00

BAIRD CLOCKS
5c VERSION 1894 -1896

NOTE: The 5c Coca-Cola Baird Clock seems to be rarer than the earlier "Relieves Exhaustion" version. Below are three different examples of these clocks, it is most likely that they were changed year by year.

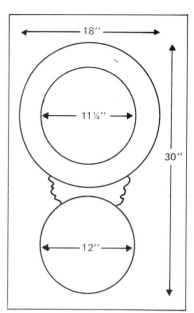

Dimensions of the Figure "8" clock.

$3,800.00

$3,800.00

$3,800.00

NOTE: Clocks are always more desirable when found with the original label. This label is pasted on the inside back-board of the clock and can be seen by opening the bottom door. Below is one example of the many different I've seen.

CLOCKS

Note: Faded red ink is very common on these clock faces.

1901 Welch Octagon School House Clock "E.N. Welch Mfg., Co., Forestville, Conn. (2 different examples shown) with "Hilda Clark" cardboard insert and 1901 calendar (top portion) insert.

Rare when found complete.
with insert $3,000.00
without insert . . $1,800.00

Note: The Ingraham Clocks shown here have original bottom glass marked "Regulator" I have never seen these clocks, which I consider original, with any other bottom glass.

1903 - 1905
Ingraham Octagon Schoolhouse
Mfg. by The E. Ingraham Co.
Bristol, Conn. $1,750.00

1905 - 1907 Ingraham Store Regulator
Mfg. by The E. Ingraham Co., Bristol, Conn.
$1,750.00

CLOCKS (STORE REGULATORS)

NOTE: These store regulators are the easiest clocks for the unsuspecting collector to get stuck with. Reproduction faces and bottom glass are easily available, especially among clock collectors and dealers. These faces can be put on legitimate old regulator clocks which are worth a couple of hundred dollars, and turn them into the much sought after Coca-Cola clock. Remember it is very common for the red printing on these faces to be faded. Dark red printed faces should be examined very carefully. The words "Trade Mark" or "Trade Mark Registered" should NOT be under the logo. The gold painted bottom glass should look a little crude. If it is too perfect, be cautious.

1910 GILBERT $2,500.00

The bottom of this clock is a decal on glass. The condition of that decal is most important when evaluating the clock. If the decal is poor the price will drop considerably.

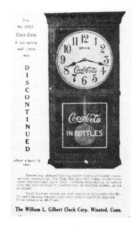

1941 Postcard $35.00

Postcard from The Gilbert Clock Co. to Coca-Cola bottlers notifying them of the discontinued manufacturing of the No. 3022 8 day clock.

1916-1920 GILBERT . . $850.00

1916-1920 GILBERT . . $1,000.00

1931 Catalog Sheet showing not only the electric clock but the regulator. . . $30.00

GILBERT $850.00

This clock was first offered in the late 20's and used through the 1930's and still available until 1941.

-146-

CLOCKS

c.1910 LEATHER 3''X8''
$500.00

c.1910 LEATHER 4½''X6''
$500.00

1950's ''DOME CLOCK'' 6''X 9''
$800.00

1950's ''DOME CLOCK'' 3''X 5''
$400.00

c.1939-41 WOOD FRAME 16''X16''
$450.00

c.1939-41 METAL FRAME 16''X16''
$400.00

c.1942 METAL FRAME 16''X16''
$325.00

1939 WOOD FRAME 16''X16''
$225.00

c.1950's $275.00

1958 . . . . $95.00

1951 MAROON 17½'' . . $60.00

1951 SILVER 17½'' . . $75.00

c.1939-41 METAL FRAME . . $385.00

EARLY ELECTRIC 8'' . . $425.00

c.1948 19'' . . . $65.00

CLOCKS

c.1941 Octagon 18'' Neon
$750.00

c.1942 Sessions 14½''X 14½'' . . $325.00

1970's $40.00

1980 Sessions $350.00

Numbered Limited Edition, time & strike
8 day movement. Presented by
Coca-Cola USA for sales excellence.

1920's Pocket Watch $750.00

NOTE: *This is one of the very few*
Coca-Cola pocket watches that I
consider old and completely original.

Photo Courtesy: The Rentzer Family Collection

1950's $75.00

1981 Ridgeway Anniversary Clock
12'' battery operated . . . $125.00

CLOCKS

c.1915 Leather
3¼''X3¼'' $400.00

c.1931 14''X 14'' This is one of the first electric
Coca-Cola Clocks $425.00

1950's Cooler Clock/Radio
Bottom photo shows clock
instruction label on bottom
of case $575.00

1950's Plastic . . . $85.00

1950's Light - up (glass front) . . . $275.00

1970's Battery Operated
¾ Size 12''X27'' . . . $150.00

1960's . . . $60.00
White & Red

1960's Plastic Light up . . . $85.00

1960's Plastic . . . $35.00

1948 36'' . . . $100.00

1970's Plastic . . . $35.00

CLOCKS

1950's (German) Dome Clock . . $375.00

1950's (German) Desk Clock . . $175.00

1970's Plastic $20.00

1950's 15''X 24'' Metal and plastic $125.00

1960's $60.00

1980's Plastic $15.00

1970's Plastic $35.00

1970's Tab (plastic) $20.00

1980's $20.00

1980's $15.00

CLOCKS

1960 . . . $75.00

1960's $60.00

1960's $55.00
Green/Red/White

1963 Plastic . . . $45.00

1960's Plastic . . . $30.00

1970's Plastic . . . $20.00

1974 Betty, Plastic . . . $35.00

1972 Plastic . . . $40.00

1970's Plastic . . . $20.00

RADIOS

1950 COOLER RADIO 7"X12"X9½" $450.00

1933 30" BOTTLE RADIO . $1,500.00

1970's VENDING MACHINE SHAPED . . . $75.00

NOTE: There is also a "Clock-Radio" version of this cooler. It can be found in the "Clock" section of this book.

c.1950's RADIO IN A CASE RARE $375.00

c.1960's VENDING MACHINE SHAPED SMALL SIZE $175.00

1965 VENDING MACHINE SHAPED LARGE SIZE $100.00

c.1963 VENDING MACHINE SHAPED $85.00

METALCRAFT TRUCKS

NOTE: 1930's Metalcraft trucks are 11" long. Considered rare when found in original box. Keep in mind the prices listed here are for trucks in nice condition. Paint chips, pitting, and decal wear can effect the value drastically.

Metalcraft No. 215 with rubber wheels and working headlights
Mint in original box $1,200.00
NOTE: Beware of reproduction of this box.

Metalcraft No. 171 with rubber wheels
Mint in original box $1,100.00

RUBBER WHEELS $375.00

RUBBER WHEELS WITH
WORKING HEADLIGHTS . . . $425.00

LONG FRONT (RUBBER WHEELS)
RARE $750.00

METAL WHEELS $350.00

TOY TRUCKS

c.1940
Buddy L 19''
wood . . . . Rare $1,500.00

c.1960 Ford station wagon, Tin
red and white 5½'' Rare $275.00

c.1950 GMC (green, yellow, white)
5½'' Rare $500.00

1950's Linemar, Tin 5'' $250.00

c.1960's Micro Models (International)
4'' Rare $175.00

1960 Ice Cream Truck, Tin wind-up
4½'' Rare $375.00

c.1950's "HAJI" Tin Litho
4¼'' (made in Japan) $200.00

c.1970 Europa VW pick up
(battery operated) 4½'' $60.00

c.1960 Micro Models "Holden Van"
Plastic 4'' Rare $175.00

-154-

TOY TRUCKS

1950's Budgie $165.00

1950's Battery operated 2 different examples
yellow/white . . . . $100.00   (with original box)   red/white $150.00

1950's Tippco 9'' $375.00
(in original box)

1950 Marx plastic (2 different examples) . . . . . . $175.00 Each
(When complete with side doors)

c.1965 Dinky . . $40.00

1950's
Friction . . $75.00

1950's Linemar . . . $85.00

1950's Plastic (French) . . . $375.00

1960 Pick up with cardboard insert . . . $300.00

c.1960 plastic . . $45.00

c.1960 Matchbox . . $50.00

1973 Big Wheel . . . $35.00

1970's plastic $25.00

1970's Model T Van kit . . $25.00

TOY TRUCKS AND TRAINS

1950's Plastic . . $45.00

c.1950 AMF (Italy) Tin Litho-plastic wheels 3¾'' $425.00

c.1960 Matchbox . . $35.00

1950's 4'' $75.00

1940's Friction $100.00

1960's $55.00

1950's Buddy L (Orange)
Deluxe Model $225.00

1960's Train Car . . $25.00

1970's (Japan) Double Decker Bus . . $65.00

1950's Toy Hot Dog Wagon . . . $125.00
Without Box $50.00

1970's Lionel Train Set
Complete in Box $85.00

1950's Marx $325.00
(Mint in original box)

TOY TRUCKS AND CARS

Late 40's Smith-Miller (Wood & Metal) $425.00

Early 50's Smith-Miller $350.00

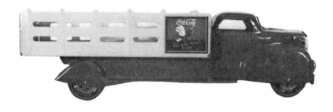

1940's Sprite Boy (Red & Yellow) $175.00

1960's Buddy L $100.00
(Mint in original box)

Early 50's Buddy L $85.00

1960's Buddy L $50.00

1970's Nylint 18 Wheeler . . . $35.00

1950's Sprite Boy $125.00

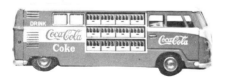

1950's VW Van $100.00

1950's VW Van (Small size)
$75.00

1960's Friction Car $100.00
(Mint in original Box)

TOY TRUCKS

c.1950 Tin $150.00

c.1973 Big Wheel . . $25.00

1950's MARX (Mint in original box) 2 different examples . . . . $200.00 Each

1950's MARX plastic $275.00
(Mint in original box)

c.1956 Tin Friction $175.00

1960 Pick up (without cardboard insert piece)
$175.00

1940's LINCOLN $400.00
(Rare when found with original wood cases)

1950's Sprite Boy $125.00

1950's MARX $125.00

Late 40's Sprite Boy (Yellow) $200.00

1950's Tin Wind Up Double Decker Bus and Terminal in Box $250.00

TOY TRUCKS

1950's GOSO wind up 8¼'' Rare $475.00

c.1949 GOSO wind up 8¼'' Rare $500.00
In original box Very Rare $1,000.00

1950's Marx (Mint in original box) $325.00

c.1950 Buddy L (Mint in original box) . . $175.00

c.1965 Dinky Toy (Mint in original box) . . $150.00

c.1978 Smith Miller (Mint in original box)
$395.00

c.1950 8½'' Rare $250.00

c.1958 Matchbox
Even load $75.00

c.1953 Matchbox
Staggered load . . $100.00

c.1960 Matchbox . . $50.00

c.1950 Bembrose U.K.
2½'' Rare $100.00
(Matchbox copy)

c.1960 Fishtail 2¼''
$75.00

1970's
Nostalgic Miniature
2'' $35.00

1960's Wiking
1½'' plastic
(Germany) $35.00

c.1948 AMF (Italy) Tin litho - Tin wheels
3¾'' Rare
$450.00

c.1960 5'' Tin litho (Japan)
Rare $275.00

1970's Tin/Plastic
(Japan) . . $75.00

1970's Tin/Plastic 3½''
$8.00 - $12.00
(6 different variations)

c.1983 Ralstoy 4¼'' . . $20.00

1970's (Spain) plastic 4¾'' . . $50.00

1970's (Hong Kong) Friction 5½'' plastic
$25.00

TOY TRUCKS, ETC.

c.1950 Marx No. 21 (Canadian version) . . $450.00

c.1960 Milton Toy Rare . . . $100.00

1980 3½'' plastic $20.00

1960's Van 8½'' (Mint in original box) . . . $100.00

1970's wind up (Japan) . . . $60.00

1970's Race Car Pillow 15'' $45.00

1970's Trolley (Spain) 6¼'' . . . $65.00

1980's VW bank and VW lighter 4¼'' . . . . $35.00 Each

TOY TRUCKS

c.1938 (Italian) Wood, Tin and Bakelite
Very Rare $900.00

1950's Marx (Plastic)
Mint in original box $325.00
Without box $150.00

1970's Buddy-L Racer
2½" $20.00

Date Unkown Tin Litho 1½"
Rare $225.00

c.1960 (France) Sesame
Plastic & Tin 4" Friction
2 different colors . . $100.00 Each

c.1970 (Japan) Plastic & Tin
Friction $30.00

c.1980 Yaxon (Italian) 12½" Die-Cast
3 color variations $150.00

TOY TRUCKS, ETC.

c.1960 Wiking (Germany)
plastic 3½″ $75.00

c.1960 Spanish 2¾″ plastic
Rare $100.00

c.1980 Tomica, Dandy VW 4″ . . . $75.00

c.1980 M.T.I. Route Truck 4″ . . $50.00

c.1970 Dinky, plastic (Hong Kong)
6½″ $20.00

c.1960 Assorted Van set (Complete set of 12
vans in box) $300.00

c.1970 Van, (Mexico) plastic
4″ Rare $75.00

c.1950 Train, tin wind-up 4 pieces, 14″ Rare . . . $150.00

Recent Diet Coke, Playart
metal 2½″ . . . $25.00

1980's Scania (Brazil) plastic 5″ $25.00

c.1960 Sesame (France) 6″
part of set $100.00

c.1960's Peugeot (France) 4'' Rare . . . . . $125.00 Each

c.1980 Tomica (Japan) 2½'' . . $50.00

c.1969 GMC (Mexico) plastic 7¼'' Rare . . $150.00

c.1970 Tente (Mexico) . . $15.00

1980's Scania (Brazil) metal 7'' $35.00

c.1970's Renaults (France) M.T.I.
4'' (yellow & red versions) . . $35.00 Ea.

c.1980's Saurer (Germany) plastic 5¼'' $10.00

1980's Renaults (France)
(metal & plastic versions) . . $30.00 Ea.

1980 Jirapuru (Brazil) Ford Route Truck
plastic 7¼'' $25.00

TOY TRUCKS
(foreign)

1970's VW Lemy (Mexico) $75.00

1950's VW Tippco (Germany) 9'' $375.00

c.1950 Schildkroet (Germany) plastic 15½'' Rare $200.00

1970 VW Gama (Germany) 4¼'' . . . $150.00

1960's VW Gama (Germany) 4'' . . . $125.00

1970's Jumbo Trailer 16'' (Japan) $75.00

1960's Stradair (France) 4'' $200.00

1980's (Japan) plastic 12'' $45.00

1960's Tigre 2000 (Spain) 13¾'' $150.00

TOYS AND GAMES

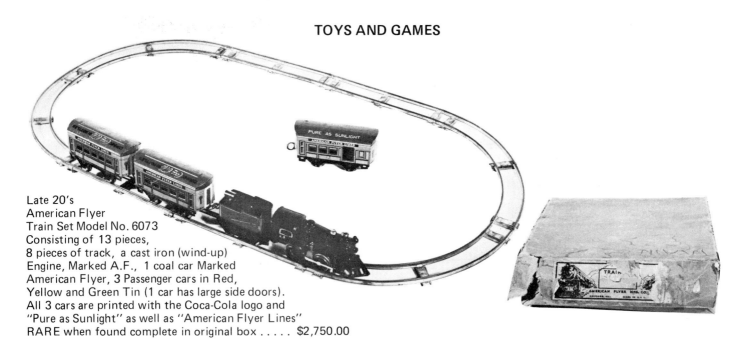

Late 20's
American Flyer
Train Set Model No. 6073
Consisting of 13 pieces,
8 pieces of track, a cast iron (wind-up)
Engine, Marked A.F., 1 coal car Marked
American Flyer, 3 Passenger cars in Red,
Yellow and Green Tin (1 car has large side doors).
All 3 cars are printed with the Coca-Cola logo and
"Pure as Sunlight" as well as "American Flyer Lines"
RARE when found complete in original box $2,750.00

INDIVIDUAL "AMERICAN FLYER" TRAIN CARS $750.00

1970's Tyco Kit (Drug Store)
for train set $20.00

1970's Lima Train Car . . $15.00

1950's "Playtown" Hamburger Stand . . $85.00

1950's "Railroad Set" cardboard set-up for train set
with Coca-Cola billboard $50.00

1950's "Hamburger Stand"
$50.00

TOYS AND GAMES

1950's Toy Shopping Basket
$125.00

1930-31 8"X 10" photo, St. Louis Bottling Plant.
"The Premium Room" showing many Coca-Cola
scooters, wagons, etc. $35.00

1930-31

"Coca-Cola Flyer"
(3 wheel scooter)

on front fork
"Save Coca-Cola crowns - get one"

36" long, Rare $2,000.00

Photo Courtesy: Ron Paradoski
St. Louis, Mo.

1960 Bottle Case Wagon
in box $125.00
without box . . . $45.00

1970's Kiddy-Car (plastic) . . . $45.00

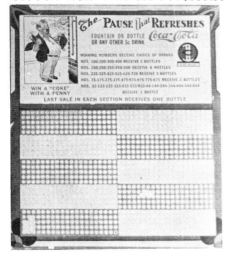

1930's 9¼"X 9¼" Punchboard . . $300.00

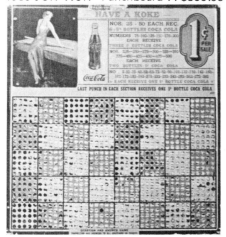

1930's 9¼"X 9¼" Punchboard . . $300.00

1930's 9¼"X 9¼" Punchboard . . $300.00

1940's 5¼"X 6½" Punch Card . . $25.00

c.1916 "Household Words Game"
card game (48 cards) each with a different product on the face.
Coke, Orange Crush, Wrigley's Gum, Etc.
Rare $150.00

c.1941 "The Coke Crowd" Paper Dolls Cutout Book
Printed by Merrill Co., Publishers Chicago, Ill.
Rare $175.00

TOYS AND GAMES

c.1950 "Paddle Ball"
(local bottler) $35.00

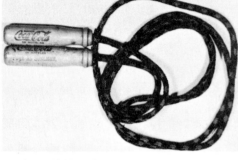

Late 1920's "Pure as Sunlight"
Jump Rope $175.00
(Have also seen this Jump Rope
with whistle in handle)

1930's
American Flyer
Kite $225.00

NOTE:
Many times
local bottlers
would give away
items without using
the standard "Coca-Cola"
logo, but rather a different
type style. These items are
still collectible but generally
are not as desirable.

1950's Marbles $30.00

Late 1940's Marbles . . . $30.00

1930's Yo-Yo . . . $50.00

1970's
Yo-Yo
$4.00

1960's
Yo-Yo
$10.00

c.1950's Golf Ball $20.00

c.1950's "Sprite Boy" wood,
ring toss game $75.00

1970's Baseball . $10.00

1970's
Yo-Yo
$4.00

1930's Wooden "Top" Game $50.00

1970's Bat (Aluminum) $25.00

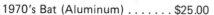

c.1968 Bat (Wood) $50.00

TOYS AND GAMES

Late 1920's
Bang Gun . . $30.00

1950's
Bang Gun . . . $15.00

1950's (Dayton) "Smile"
game cards . . . $40.00 Each

1950's
Clicker Pistol
$20.00

1970's
Bang Gun . . $3.00

1980's Santa
"Ring Toss"
$5.00

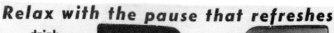

Relax with the pause that refreshes
drink Coca-Cola in bottles

1950's 3-D Glasses $30.00

1960's Pop Corn bag
$5.00

1932 Puzzle (wood)
Rare $450.00

1940's "Coca-Cola Commandos"
cutouts $125.00

1960's Pop Corn box
$8.00

1950's "Rootie Kazootie" pop-out puppets
carton stuffers . . $6.00 ea. $30.00 set

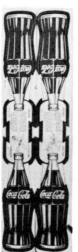

c.1950 Boomerang . $7.00

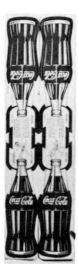

1980's "Stunt Plane"
$10.00

GAMES

1940's Cribbage Board . . . $45.00

1941 Game Set (in original box) $175.00

1940's - 50's Darts $25.00
(darts not marked with logo)

1940's
Dominos $40.00

1950's Shanghai Game . . $15.00

1940's
Checkers . . . $35.00

1930's Coca-Cola Punching Ball Game (complete in box with mask and ball) Rare . . . $400.00

1940's Dart Board . . . $45.00

1940's Chinese Checkers . . $60.00

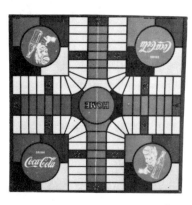

1940's - 50's Parcheesi Game . . $40.00

TOYS AND GAMES

c.1910-1916 Whistle 6¼''
(cardboard) shown open . . $300.00

(Inside of Whistles shown
at left and right)

c.1916-1920 Whistle 5¾''
(cardboard) shown open . . $250.00

c.1920's Whistle 3¾''
(Cardboard) . . $175.00

c.1920's Clicker
(metal) . . $100.00

1920'S Whistle (tin) . $60.00

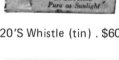

1930's Clicker
(metal) . . $60.00

1920's Whistle (wood) . . $50.00

c.1950 Whistle (plastic) . . $10.00

1930's Siren
Whistle . $30.00

1930's Whistle
(tin) . . $75.00

c.1930's "Machine Gun Bubble Blower"
with instructions, Rare $175.00

Early 1960's Kazoo. . . $50.00

(probably a local bottler piece)

c.1950 Crystal Radio Set
with instructions . . $150.00

c.1930's Play Moustache (heavy paper cutout)
"Roanoake Coca-Cola Bott. Works, Inc." . . $25.00

c.1957 Eddie Fisher "Charm Bracelet" . . $75.00

c.1920 Dice Set (5) in leather case . . $125.00

TOYS AND GAMES

1970's Pillow $8.00

c.1950 Pillow . . . $50.00

1950's Bingo Card . . $3.00

1930's Bingo Card . . $25.00

1960's Hi-Jacs $10.00
(cloth bottle covers)

1960 Plastic (blow-up)
Can $10.00

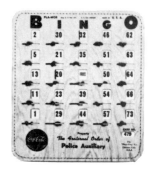

1960's Magic Kit . . $50.00

1941 Bingo Card . . . $25.00

1950's "Dolly Loves A Party"
set $60.00

1950's "Dolly Picnic Set" . . . $60.00

1980's Cobot $60.00

1950's "Tour the World"
Coke bottle cap set $50.00

c.1964 "Bo Lyn's Flip Football" Game $20.00

Dominos $30.00

Jigsaw Puzzle $45.00

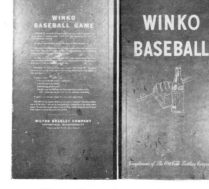

Winko Baseball $50.00

Bingo Set $45.00

Ring Toss $65.00

Table Tennis Set $45.00
(paddles marked with logo)

Checkers . . . $30.00

Darts $25.00
(darts not marked with logo)

Jigsaw Puzzle . . . $45.00

Game Set $50.00

Tower of Hannoi Game, Rare $85.00

Broadsides Game . . . $50.00

Game Set $165.00
(2 decks of cards, cribbage
board, dominos, checkers)

Chess Set . . . $45.00

Checkers, Backgammon $75.00

Horse Race Game, Rare $175.00

DOLLS

c.1950's Buddy Lee Doll 12"
Composition $500.00
Plastic $250.00

NOTE: These values are for dolls with original uniforms. Reproduction uniforms are common. Be Careful!

1950's - 1960's
COCA-COLA SANTA DOLLS

White Boots $60.00

NOTE: The "Santa Doll", quite frankly has never been my favorite piece of Coca-Cola advertising. I have seen these dolls sell for more than my estimated values, however I just don't feel they are worth it. I have also seen quite a few different variations and do consider some of them questionable.

Black Santa $50.00

Black Boots . $60.00

1960's Santa . . . $25.00

Santa with Coca-Cola (label) belt buckle. Questionable

White Boots . . . $60.00

1960's Santa (with caution tag) $45.00

SCHOOL STUFF

c.1930's Pencil Box (Complete with 10 pieces) $30.00

1940's School Package
Envelope only $5.00
Complete package . . . $20.00

1930's School Package
Envelope only $5.00
Complete package . . $30.00

1950's School Package (Complete with 4 pieces including envelope) . . . $15.00

1930's Pencil Sharpeners. . . $25.00 Each
Complete box of 12 . . . . . . $325.00

c.1929 School Package
Envelope only . . $10.00
Complete Package . . . $50.00

1940's School Package
Envelope only $5.00
Complete package . . $20.00

1930's Game of "Safety & Danger" (Canada) showing both sides . . . $75.00

1938
Game of "Steps to Health" (Canada) $75.00
This game came in an unmarked envelope, along with game piece and die.

RULERS

1950's "Fishing Ruler" $8.00

Western Coca-Cola $20.00

1940's $5.00

NOTE: *Rulers were produced and given away in such large quantities that most are very common.*

"Golden Rule" (showing both sides) $1.00
This is the most common ruler, produced from the late 1920's into the 1960's. If dated $2.00

1950's $4.00

1950's-60's Mexican $3.00

1970's $2.00

1980 Jackson, Tenn. $2.00

Late 1950's English $7.00

1973 Houston Astro's (plastic) $7.00

Pencil Box Ruler . . . $2.00

1970's (plastic) $3.00

1980's (plastic) $1.00

1970's (plastic) $2.00

1982 Corinth, Miss. $2.00

1967 Piqua, Oh. (plastic) $4.00

"Golden Rule" Yard Stick $6.00

1950's Yard Stick $6.00

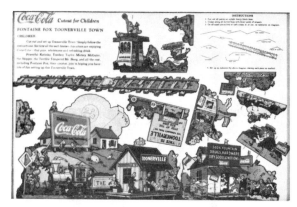

TOONERVILLE TOWN $165.00

1929 "CORNER STORE" $65.00

1932 "OLYMPICS" $35.00

1927 "CIRCUS" $50.00

1932 "CIRCUS" (with glass) $35.00

1932 "CIRCUS" (with bottle) $65.00

1927 "TOY TOWN" $50.00

1931 "UNCLE REMUS" $200.00

NOTE: These cutouts are 10''X 15'' printed on lightweight cardstock. They were given away to children, at the same time the corresponding window display was in the store window. There was also a window banner with each display informing the children of the free cutouts.

SALESMAN SAMPLE COOLERS

NOTE: 1929 Glascock Salesman Sample Coolers found with original carrying case would certainly be worth more.

1929 GLASCOCK
"SINGLE CASE" 5½"X5½"X10½"
RARE $2,900.00

1929 GLASCOCK
"DOUBLE CASE" 8"X10½"X13" . . . $2,500.00

NOTE: 1939 Salesman Sample Coolers came equipped with a group of pages entitled "A Business Builder", attached by a ring binder on the inside of lid. These pages show the different coolers available. The cooler is much more interesting and desirable when found with these pages. The "Closed Front" is actually a snap on piece that goes onto the "Open Front" cooler.

1939 "CLOSED FRONT" 8½"X11"X9" $850.00

1939 "OPEN FRONT" 8½"X11"X9" $750.00

NOTE: 1939 Salesman Sample Coolers found with original carrying case would certainly be worth more.

SALES AIDS, MINIATURES, TOY DISPENSERS

1970's Toy Dispenser
In box
$20.00

1950's Dispenser Bank $125.00
Mint in original box $250.00

1960's
Dispenser Bank
plastic $50.00

1950's Vending Machine Bank
plastic 5½" $65.00

1950's Miniature Sales Aid . . . $75.00

1960's Toy Dispenser (plastic) $30.00

1950's Toy Dispenser (plastic) $45.00

MINIATURES

1950's Plastic Vending
Machine Bank $100.00

1930's Wood Case . . . $65.00

1950's 2 Different examples . . . $35.00 Each

1960's Plastic Case . . $35.00

Wood Cooler 4"X7"X4½"
This could have been a
salesmans sample . . . $125.00

1950's Plastic Mini Picnic Cooler
w/bottles $45.00

1950's . . . $35.00

1970's Plastic Case and Bottles . $10.00

1930's . . . $50.00

1960's Dispenser Bank . . $85.00
(Mint in box)

1950's Mexico
Tin Carrier with
embossed bottles . . . $45.00

1960's . . . $10.00

1950's Plastic Case . . $35.00

Bottles have long been a favorite among collectors of Coca-Cola memorabilia. A fascinating variety of styles, shapes and colors were used down through the years, although most collections seem to center around the different cities where Coca-Cola bottling franchises have existed.

The earliest bottles know to contain Coca-Cola were of the Hutchinson stoppered variety. The words **Coca-Cola** appear in either block print or script lettering on the bottles and embossing usually designated the city where the bottle was originally filled as well. These Hutchinson bottles were used only briefly by fewer than a dozen bottling works just after the turn of the century. Relatively few have survived.

Crown-top, straight-sided bottles replaced the heavier, cruder Hutchinson bottles in the early 1900's. Literally millions of these crown-top bottles were used by the ever-increasing number of Coca-Cola franchises between 1902 and 1915. Few records were kept, however, and individualism was rampant. A given Coca-Cola bottling works might use bottles of several different styles and colors at various times. Some bottles had fancy designs such as rings, shields or arrows embossed onto the glass; still others had slug plates identifying the then proprietor of the Coca-Cola franchise. All of these straight-sided bottles displayed a paper label identifying the product they contained and bore the Coca-Cola trademark embossed in script lettering as well.

The early crown-top bottles were hand blown in molds with their necks and lips finished off by special hand-held tools. Such techniques often left rough seams, irregular patterns of thick and thin glass, numerous bubbles and imperfections in the glass itself, and sometimes crooked shapes. Machine-made crown-top bottles with fewer deficiencies and evenly formed seams began to replace the hand-tooled bottles after 1910. The variety of glass colors used ranged from clear and aqua to differing shades of blue, green and amber. Even the amount of liquid a bottle contained varied considerably since 6, 6½, 7 up to quart-size 24 and 26 ounce bottles existed. The script writing Coca-Cola trademark appeared sometimes at the base of the bottle, sometimes in the center, sometimes up on the shoulder. While this tremendous lack of uniformity makes for some interesting collections of straight-sided Coca-Cola bottles, the inevitable confusion generated by such diversity eventually led to the adoption of the now famous "hobbleskirt" or "Mae West" shaped bottle as the standard glass container for Coca-Cola shortly after 1915.

The first patent for these hobbleskirt bottles was issued on Nov. 16, 1915 to the Chapman Root Glass company of Terre Haute, Indiana. This patent was renewed on Dec. 25, 1923. Such "Thanksgiving" or "Christmas" Cokes, as they are sometimes called, have become quite popular among collectors because on the base plate most of these bottles bear the name of the city where they were first filled. Well over 2,000 cities are known to have existed as the Coca-Cola bottling network continued to expand. Several patent renewals of the classic shape have occurred since 1923. Hundreds of millions of hobbleskirt bottles were put into service over the years.

Many bottles can be found on which the words **Coca-Cola** or **property of Coca-Cola** appear in block letter print only. Although some of these bottles are of the older, hand blown variety, most date from the 1920's or later. Collectors generally agree that these block letter bottles probably contained the various fruit flavored drinks that were handled by individual bottling franchises rather than the beverage Coca-Cola itself. Often these bottles had paper labels identifying the kind of soda water they contained. Larger, quart-size bottles were also used in this way. These "block letter" bottles come in a great variety of colors and shapes and make for an interesting collection in and of themselves. A surprising number have fancy embossings such as people or animals. But once again, it is important to remember that very few, if any at all, were ever used for Coca-Cola. Keep in mind that these "flavor bottles" generally **do not** have the value of bottles that actually contained Coca-Cola.

Two other types of bottles deserve mention when writing about Coca-Cola bottle collections. Syrup bottles did indeed contain genuine Coca-Cola syrup obtained from the parent company in Atlanta and used at sit-down soda fountains to hand mix one's 5¢ drink with carbonated water. Many of these tall, clear glass bottles have the words **Coca-Cola** in acid-etched lettering or printed on paper labels sometimes sealed under glass. The trademark appears on such bottles in block lettering or in script.

Certain Coca-Cola franchises also bottled and sold seltzer water to local outlets such as bars, restaurants and soda fountains. This was done in a variety of beautifully colored or clear glass siphon bottles that had acid-etched lettering or applied color labeling. The words **Coca-Cola** are found on these bottles in both block letter or script writing, although such bottles were used for seltzer water only and never to dispense Coca-Cola itself.

The relative value placed upon Coca-Cola bottles is determined in great part by such factors as the age of the bottle (Hutchinson, straight-sided, hobbleskirt), its scarcity (small town versus large franchise, for example), and also the color of the glass and condition of the bottle itself (free from chips, cracks, cloudiness or considerable wear). An original metal crown or paper label would enhance the value of a Coca-Cola bottle appreciably.

BOTTLES
HUTCHINSONS

SCRIPT . . $675.00

BLOCK . . $475.00

Biedenharn Candy
$125.00
(not marked Coca-Cola)

1961 Commemorative
$100.00

STRAIGHT SIDED BOTTLES

Biedenharn
with label . . $145.00

Best by a Dam Site
$50.00

Biedenharn
$100.00

Clear with Label
$75.00

Amber with Label
$125.00

Diamond Amber
$75.00

1971 Root
Commorative
Bottle

Bottle Only
$75.00

Bottle With
Hanger $125.00

Complete
in Box $175.00

I break down the catagories of bottles as follows:

Hutchinsons, Rare and unusual Ambers, Paper labels etc.	As shown above
Straight Side Ambers , depending on state & town	$35.00 - $150.00
Straight Side Ambers with Arrows, depending on state & town .	$45.00 - $175.00
Straight Side Clear, Green, or Aqua	$15.00 - $ 35.00
Hobble-Skirt, 1915 version, depending on state	$ 2.00 - $ 10.00
Hobble-Skirt, 1923 Xmas Coke, ...	$ 1.00 - $ 5.00
Hobble-Skirt, Pat. D version	.50 - $ 1.00
Hobble-Skirt, ACL version	.10 - .50
Coca-Cola Flavor bottles, (Big Chief, Royal Palm, etc.)	$ 2.00 - $ 10.00

BOTTLES

Script logo 30 oz.
Rochester, NY
Light Blue . . . $150.00

Script logo, quart size
Wyanoke Brand
Light Green $150.00

Block type logo, quart size
The Northern Coca-Cola
Bott. Co. Kalamazoo, Mich.
Light Green $100.00

Block type logo, 24 oz.
Coca-Cola Bottling Co.
Westminster, MD
Clear $100.00

FLAVOR BOTTLES (Coca-Cola Bottling Co.)

J.S. Francis, Avon Park Fla. 6oz.
Dark Green and Light Green examples . . $3.00 Each

Big Chief
Embossed Indian Head
Light Green . . . $6.00

Quality Brand Soda Water
Asheville, NC 6oz.
Light Green $3.00

NOTE: Flavor bottles did not hold Coca-Cola, but
rather other flavors bottled by local bottlers.

DISPLAY BOTTLES

c.1920's 36'' Leaded Glass,
Display Bottle $6,000.00

1920's 26'' Bottle Lamp $2,000.00

NOTE: This is a variation glass bottle lamp.
The differences being, size, style of cap, a
completely different un-marked base, and no
marking under the logo.

1920's 20'' Bottle Lamp $2,200.00

1930's 20'' Glass (Christmas Coke)
Display Bottle $175.00

20'' Glass Display Bottles (not shown)

Pat. D version $150.00
ACL (applied color lettering) . $ 85.00
ACL Mexico . . . . $ 65.00

Display bottles found with
original cap, would certainly
increase there value.

1953 20'' Plastic $275.00

c.1961 42'' Styrofoam . . $175.00

SYRUP BOTTLES

Early 1900's
Label under glass . . $475.00

Early 1900's
Label under glass . . . $675.00

c.1920's
Label under glass . . . $300.00

c.1920's $375.00

c.1910 . . . . . . $325.00

c.1920's $250.00

SELTZER BOTTLES

Coca-Cola (Block lettering) Seltzer Bottles

$125.00 $125.00 $125.00 $125.00

ACL - Applied Color Labeling

$100.00 $85.00 $250.00 $100.00

SELTZER BOTTLES

ACL $85.00

Red ACL $295.00

Denver, Co. (Blue) . . . $275.00

Red ACL . . . $150.00

1940's ACL . . . $65.00

Denver, Co. (Clear) . . . $260.00 Each

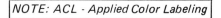

NOTE: ACL - Applied Color Labeling

SELTZER BOTTLES

Billings, Mt. (Clear) . . . $275.00

NOTE: Dating these bottles is very difficult, most were in use for many years.

Red ACL . . . $250.00

$125.00

$125.00

c.1940's . $85.00

$125.00

$295.00 $125.00 $95.00

1940's . $85.00

ROYAL PALM SELTZER

1930's-40's . $85.00 Each

Chicago, Ill. (Clear) $250.00 Each

$85.00 $150.00

NOTE: Seltzer Bottles with script logos as opposed to block type have more value.

$125.00

SYRUP CONTAINERS

1930's Glass Jug with Paper Label
$65.00

Early 1900's Ceramic Syrup Jug
with Paper Label
as shown $100.00
with Near Mint Label . $475.00

Late 1940's 5 Gal. Syrup Can
Paper Label on Lid $100.00

1914 - 1919 Glass Syrup Jug, with 2 Paper Labels
showing both sides $150.00

1960's Cardboard
Syrup Container . . $10.00

Late 1930's Can with Paper Label
$65.00

1970's One Gallon Tin Can . . . . . $8.00 Each

1930's Cardboard Box for Syrup Jug $35.00

SYRUP BOTTLES AND KEGS

1950's . . $10.00 Ea. Full Case . . $45.00

1920's SYRUP JUGS . . . . $65.00 EACH

> NOTE: The quality of the paper label on these jugs is very important when determining value.

1940's $45.00

1950's $15.00

1960 . . . . $8.00

1960's . . $5.00 Ea. Full Case . . $25.00

Late teens, wood syrup kegs
(5 GAL.)
2 Different Examples
$75.00 Each

(As the quality of the paper label
goes down so does the value.)

GLASSES

c.1900-1904 Straight Sided
$500.00

c.1912 (Large 5c) Flare
$450.00
c.1912-1913 (Small 5c) not shown . $550.00

c.1916 ("Bottle") Flare
Rare . . $350.00

c.1923-1927 Modified Flare
$75.00

NOTE: At least 3 different
varieties of this glass exist, with
different syrup lines or trademark
in tail.

c.1929-1940 Bell Shape
$30.00
(trademark in tail)

c.1941-1946 Bell Shape
ACL (trademark below script) . $10.00

NOTE: Later variations (with "Drink",
"Enjoy" and "Coke") not shown
values . . $1.00 to $5.00

c.1930's Pewter Bell Shape
with leather pouch $300.00
without leather pouch . . . $150.00

1950's 50th Anniversary, Gold Dipped, ACL
(with plastic display stand)
8oz. and 6oz. . . . . $50.00 Each

Early 1900's Flare Glass
"Moriarty & Neil"
Rare $500.00

Early 1900's Silver Glass Holder
Take Note the word "DRINK" Does Not appear on the original
RARE $850.00

1970's Reproduction (Pewter Type Material) Glass Holder
Take Note the word "DRINK" above Coca-Cola appears
only on the reproduction $5.00

NOTE: The Silver Glass Holder was made available to soda fountains from 1901 thru 1904. It is actually a triple plate silver over a german or nickel silver base metal. These were made to fit the straight sided glass of this period, many of which did not have the script Coca-Cola on the glass. This was a very elegant item, and shows up in some of the advertising artwork of this period. These were probably discontinued because the cost of 50c each was considered too expensive by the soda fountain operators.

1936 50th Anniversary Dinner
Glass . . . Rare $300.00
(Gold lettered, personalized glass)
Photo Courtesy: John Morgerson
Lexington, Ky.

c.1912 Coca-Cola 5c Arrow Mug
Very Rare $750.00

NOTE: Both of these mugs originated in West Virginia. The above mug is an earthen color with blue logo and design, the handle is missing on this example. The mug at left is thought to be from the Dan Mercer Pottery, and has a light green glaze. Whether these were ordered by bottlers for a specific occasion or usage or got more widespread distribution is unknown.

c.1920 Coca-Cola Embossed
Ceramic Mug
Rare $500.00

1930's Tin Water Cup $45.00
(Printing is in bottom of cup)

GLASSES, CUPS, ETC.

c.1904-1912 Flare Glass
$325.00

Akron Coca-Cola
Soap Box Derby
Glass . . . $100.00

1916-1966 (Gold) 50th Anniversary
Sommersworth, N.H. $45.00

1960 Diamond
$5.00

Coca-Cola (Canada) set of 8 tumblers
in box $85.00

1970's Wine Set . . . $20.00

1960's "Around The World" Tumblers
Complete set of 8 in box . . $85.00

1970's set of plastic tumblers
in box $15.00

1950's - 1960's case of 12 glasses in original box . . . . $45.00 Each

Cup holder (Wood) . . . $60.00

1950's . . $2.00

1960's paper cups . . . . . $2.00 Each

c.1960 Ice Bucket . . $8.00

1970's . . . $2.00

1960's . . $3.00

1950's - 70's Popcorn holders
$5.00 Each

-194-

CANS

c.1960's LARGE DIAMOND
$40.00

c.1960's BOTTLE DIAMOND
$40.00

c.1960's DIAMOND
$10.00

NOTE: These cans MUST be in beautiful condition to justify these prices. Cans that are pitted or dented, will certainly be worth less.

c.1930's SYRUP CAN $100.00

c.1950's SYRUP CAN $75.00
(Paper Label)

c.1950's SYRUP CAN $75.00
(Paper Label)

BOTTLE CARRIERS

C.1920 COCA-COLA CARDBOARD
24 BOTTLE CARRIER . . . $175.00

1924 CARDBOARD
6 PACK CARRIER
$100.00

1930's CARDBOARD
6 PACK CARRIER
$40.00

1930's CARDBOARD
6 PACK CARRIER
$25.00

1930's CARDBOARD 6 PACK CARRIERS . . . . $15.00 Each

1940's WOOD 6 PACK CARRIERS . . . . $25.00 Each

1950's ALUMINUM 6 PACK CARRIERS
$25.00 Each

1940's WOOD & MASONITE
6 PACK CARRIER
$30.00

1950's ALUMINUM
6 PACK CARRIER
$6.00

1940's MASONITE
6 BOTTLE CARRIER
$25.00

1950's CARDBOARD 12 & 6 BOTTLE CARRIERS . . . . $8.00 Each

1950's PLASTIC 8 & 6 BOTTLE CARRIERS . . . . $8.00 Each

1940's VENDORS BOTTLE CARRIER . . . $125.00

1940's AIRLINE
COOLER $85.00

BOTTLE CARRIERS

1924 . . $125.00

1924 . . . $100.00

1931 . . . $100.00

1949 . . . $20.00

1940's 4 Bottle . . . $30.00

1930's . . $30.00

1930's . . . $15.00

Late 1940's Cardboard with wire handles (3 different versions) . . . . . . $25.00 Each

1950 . . . $25.00

1949-1950 . . . $25.00

1940's . . . $25.00

1920's . . . $125.00

1950's Plastic (12 and 6 bottle) . . . . $8.00 Each

1917 48 Bottle
Wood Shipping Case
9" X 18" X 25½" $175.00

1930's 6 Pack Display Rack
(metal) complete with 8 cartons . . $500.00

BOTTLE CARRIERS

1950's . . $10.00

1950's . . $8.00

1950's . . $8.00   1960's . . $5.00

1950's 12Pack . . $8.00   1960 . . $5.00   c.1963 . . . $4.00 Each

c.1963 . . . . . $4.00 Each

Late 30's 6 Pack
Display Rack $125.00

1950's Plastic . . . $8.00 Each

Early 1900's
Syrup Bottle Case . . $100.00

1956 Cooler Bag . . $40.00

1960 Insulated
Cooler Box . . $30.00

1950's Aluminum 12 Bottle
Carrier $12.00

Early 30's 24 Bottle
Case . . $50.00

c.1920's (Dovetail)
Wood 6 Bottle
Carrier, Rare . $125.00

c.1930's
Tin/Wood
12Bottle
Case . $125.00

Early 1900's Wood Shipping Case
Very Unusual Example . . . $275.00

Vendors
Bottle Carrier . . . $60.00

BOTTLE CASES

Early wood shipping case
with lid $175.00

1920's wood $50.00

Pre-1920 wood $65.00

1940's wood $30.00

1930's wood (seltzer case) . $40.00

1930's wood $40.00

1930's wood . . . $35.00

1920's wood $50.00

1940's - 50's wood . . . $10.00

1950's wood $20.00

1940's cardboard $25.00

1950's wood $20.00

1950's cardboard $15.00

1970's cardboard $8.00

1950's - 60's plastic $15.00

1930's - 40's wire metal
English $65.00
French $50.00
(Canada)

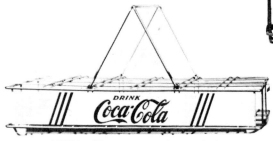

1950's - 60's wire metal $40.00

GLASCOCK COOLERS
(Standard Size)

c.1929 Single Case (Junior Size) $500.00

1929-32 Double Case (Full Size) $600.00

NOTE: These values are for coolers in choice condition. Coolers with repainted sides, and in rough condition would certainly be worth less.

There have been times when the junior size coolers have sold for a much higher price than the larger version because of it's more desirable smaller size.

c.1929 Table Top Cooler $650.00

1930's Electric (Vendor) Cooler $1,200.00

NOTE: Beware, the table top cooler must be as shown. Junior size coolers with sawed off legs are NOT table top coolers.

COOLERS AND DISPENSERS

Late 1930's (stainless steel with enamel plates)
Double Dispenser $500.00

1930's Art Deco (chrome and enamel) Dispenser
Mfg. by Multiplex Faucet Co., St. Louis, Mo.
6 sided. . . . . Rare $850.00

Late 1930's (red with chrome and enamel plates)
Dispenser $300.00

c.1939 Standard Size "Ice Cooler" (24"X 30" X 34"). . . $350.00

1950's Vendo Coin Changer (with "Have a Coke" insert). $225.00
NOTE: These machines were used in the late 1940's into the
1950's. I have seen them with inserts other than Coca-Cola.

DISPENSERS

c.1960's
Salesman's Sample
Counter Dispenser
All plastic with
Heavy Canvas
Padded Carrying Case
16½"X12" $450.00

c.1950's Vendor Dispenser
$225.00

Soda Fountain
Ceramic (Insert)
Syrup Dispenser
I've seen many different
examples of this pump dispenser . . . $65.00

COOLERS AND DISPENSERS

1960's Picnic Cooler
In original box $125.00
without box $50.00

c.1963 Picnic Cooler
In original box $100.00
without box $45.00

c.1963 Vinyl Cooler Box
$25.00

Late 1950's Barrel Dispenser $275.00

1950's Picnic Cooler
$30.00

1950's Picnic Cooler
$30.00

Early 1960's Vinyl Cooler Box
$25.00

Coin operated table top bottle dispenser
(working condition) $575.00

1960's Picnic Cooler
$30.00

SANDWICH TOASTER
Used in Soda Fountains.
(Has erroneously been called a
Krumkake Maker) $700.00

Considered Rare
Add 50% when found
in original box.

1950's Cooler Music Box $550.00
(I've seen 4 different versions of this music box)

1950's Mileage Table . . . . $150.00 Each

1920's Fire Bucket $150.00

2 Different Examples. (These Mileage Tables were
very useful and used for many years.)

1963 Bottle Shaped Book Ends (Bronze) . . $125.00

MISCELLANEOUS

Coca-Cola Barbecue Grill
In box $35.00

NOTE: Many collectors do shy away from anything with the so-called "New Logo", however some of the more unusual pieces are very collectable.

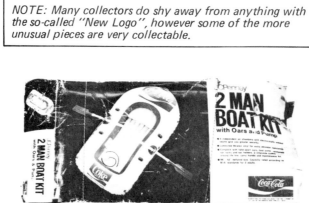

1970's 2 Man Boat Kit (inflatable)
In box $75.00

c.1960 Vinyl Cooler Bag
$35.00

1970's Stadium (plastic) seat cushion . . $7.00

c.1960 Folding Chair . . . $60.00

1970's Rug (red & white) 4'X6' $175.00

1970's Waste Paper Basket . . $10.00

1970's Tennis Racket cover
$10.00

1980's Rug (red & white) 4'X6' $100.00

POCKET MIRRORS

1920 ◄————— YEAR USED

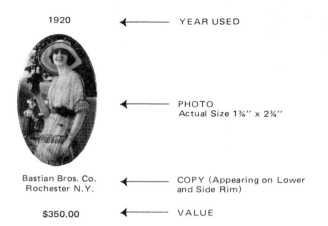

◄————— PHOTO
Actual Size 1¾" x 2¾"

Bastian Bros. Co.
Rochester N.Y.
◄————— COPY (Appearing on Lower
and Side Rim)

$350.00 ◄————— VALUE

1936 "MEMOS"
Pocket Mirrors
2 different examples
shown . . . $65.00 Each
In original
package . . $100.00

NOTE: All mirros shown (except the two at right)
are celluloid covered artwork, with a metal rim and
glass mirror on back side.

1906	1907	1908	1909	1910

The Whitehead & Hoag Co., Newark, N.J.	From the Painting Copyright 1906, by Wolf & Co. Phila.	Bastian Bros. Co. Rochester N.Y.	J.B. Carroll Chicago	J.B. Carroll Chicago
Duplicate Mirrors 5c Postage, Coca-Cola Company, Atlanta, Ga.	Bastian Bros. Co. Roch. N.Y. Duplicate Mirrors 5c Postage, Coca-Cola Company, Atlanta, Ga.	Duplicate Mirrors 5c Postage, Coca-Cola Company, Atlanta, Ga.	Duplicate Mirrors 5c Postage, Coca-Cola Company, Atlanta, Ga.	Duplicate Mirrors 5c Postage, Coca-Cola Company, Atlanta, Ga.
$300.00	$300.00	$500.00	$275.00	$200.00

1911	1914	1916	1920	1922

The Whitehead & Hoag Co. Newark, N.J.	The Whitehead & Hoag Co. Newark, N.J.	The Whitehead & Hoag Co. Newark, N.J.	Bastian Bros. Co. Rochester, N.Y.	The Whitehead & Hoag Co. Newark, N.J.
Duplicate Mirrors 5c Postage Coca-Cola Company, Atlanta, Ga.				
$200.00	$300.00	$225.00	$350.00	$800.00

Not Pictured: 1911 "Motor Girl" (formally called "Duster Girl") Pocket Mirror, oval 1 5/8"X 2 3/8". This mirror was made available by
"The Coca-Cola Bottling Company" of Atlanta, one of the parent bottlers (all of the above mirrors were issued through "The Coca-Cola Co.").
The "Motor Girl" mirror, in addition to picturing the "Motor Girl" artwork, has the copy "Drink Coca-Cola In Bottles" at bottom and "Cruver
Mfg. Co., Chicago" on left rim. Value $750.00

WATCH FOBS AND CONVENTION BADGES

Most early fobs have the manufacturers name stamped on them, but not all. A few of the fobs have been reproduced and there are a number of fantasy fobs on the market, so the novice collector should be cautious and ask the advice of advanced collectors on a questionable fob.

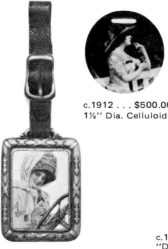

c.1913 . $600.00
1¾'' Dia. Celluloid

c.1905 . $500.00
Celluloid ''Drink
Coca-Cola in
Bottles, 5c'' on back.

c.1910 . $450.00
Celluloid ''Drink
Coca-Cola in
Bottles, 5c'' on back.

c.1912 . . . $500.00
1½'' Dia. Celluloid

1911 . . . $450.00
Celluloid ''Drink
Coca-Cola in Bottles,
5c'' on back.

c.1915 . . . $125.00
''Drink Coca-Cola in
Bottles, 5c'' on back.
(Refer to ''Swastika''
note below right)

c.1920's . . $100.00
Brass with Red Enamel.

c.1910 . . $175.00
showing both sides

c.1907 ''Relieves Fatique''

''Drink
Coca-Cola in
Bottles 5c''   ''Drink
Coca-Cola Sold
Everywhere 5c''

Brass with either Silver
or Gold Wash . . . . $100.00 Each
Sterling Silver $250.00

c.1909 . $125.00
Brass with Red
Enamel.

c.1912 . $150.00
Brass with Black
Enamel.

c.1920's . $100.00
Bulldogs 1¾''X 1¼''
''Drink Coca-Cola
Delicious and Re-
freshing 5c''on back.

c.1920's . $100.00
Bulldogs 1½''X 1''

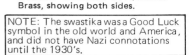

c.1920's ''Swastika'' . . . $100.00
Brass, showing both sides.

1908 Keychain $75.00

NOTE: The swastika was a Good Luck symbol in the old world and America, and did not have Nazi connotations until the 1930's.

1917 Convention
Metal with Ribbon
$400.00

1911 Convention
Badge, Celluloid
''Motor Girl'' Pin
(1¾'' Dia.) with
Ribbon. (Hyatt
Mfg. Co., Baltimore)
Rare $1,500.00

1916 Convention
Metal, Porcelain
Inlay . . . $400.00

1910 Convention
Lapel Button. $400.00

1909 Convention
Token, Brass . . $400.00
Swastika on back.
(First Bottlers Convention)

1912 Convention
Lapel Button $400.00

1915 Convention
Metal, Porcelain
Inlay . . $400.00

c.1930 Convention
Badge $75.00

1939 Convention
Badge . . . $75.00

c.1947 Convention
Badge . . . $50.00

1936 Convention
Badge . . . $75.00

c.1950 Convention
Badge . . . $50.00

c.1943 Convention
Badge . . . $50.00
Other Convention Badges also shown
in ''Miscellaneous'' section of this book.

POCKET KNIVES

An attempt is made to show mostly older knives, common and uncommon. Since the late 1960's literally hundreds of different knives marked Coca-Cola have been manufactured, in all shapes, sizes and materials. Many fantasy styles appear old and rare when "Aged", BEWARE! Refer to the "Fantasy and Reproduction pages of this book. (Knife photos courtesy of Thom Thompson)

c.1905-1915 Brass, 2 blade $300.00
Marked "A. Kaster & Co." and
"Coca-Cola Bottling Co., Germany"
Note opener on this original.

c.1905-1915 Brass 1 blade $250.00
Marked "A. Kaster & Co.", and "Coca-
Cola Bottling, Co., Germany"
Note opener on this original.

c.1905-1915 Nickel Silver $350.00
4 blades including, awl, can opener
& screw driver. Marked "D. Peres
Solingen Germany" and "Coca-Cola
Bottling Co., Germany"

c.1910 Nickel Silver, 1 blade & opener, (Both sides shown) $175.00
Marked "D. Peres, Solingen" and "Coca-Cola Bottling Co., Germany"
another example marked "Kastor & Bros." and "Coca-Cola Bottling
Co., Germany"

c.1915 Copper, 2 blades $175.00
Marked "A. Kastor & Bros., N.Y."
and Coca-Cola Bottling Co., Germany"

c.1910 Brass, 2 blade $275.00
Marked "D. Peres Solingen" and
"Coca-Cola Bottling Co., Germany"
also made in Aluminum.

c.1915-1925 Bone, $85.00
1 blade and opener. Marked
"A. Kastor & Bros. New York"
and "Coca-Cola Bottling Co."

c.1930 Stainless, 2 blade $100.00
Marked "Remington UMC" in circle.
Many stamped with bottlers name on back.

c.1940 "Serve Coca-Cola" $100.00
1 blade and nail file, pearl handle
"Be Smart" in window when open
Marked "Solingen Germany"

c.1930 Celluloid $75.00
2 blade, Marked "Shapleigh
HDW, Co."

c.1930 Stainless $100.00
2 blade, Marked "Coca-Cola Co.
Atlanta"

c.1930 Stainless $100.00
2 blade, Marked "Remington"
in circle.

c.1930 Stainless $100.00
2 blade, Marked "Coca-Cola Co.
Atlanta"

c.1930 Celluloid $50.00
2 blade, Marked "Hammer
Brand, USA"

c1930-1950 Celluloid $30.00 to $75.00
Many variations and manufactures,
"Camco USA", "Clover Brand", Etc.

c.1930 Stainless $50.00
2 blades, Most Marked
"Coca-Cola Bottling Co.
Germany"

c.1940 Stainless $30.00
2 blades(diff. mfgrs.)
when Marked "Remington" $100.00

c.1950, 1 blade plastic $10.00

1937 Switch Blade $175.00
Blade Marked "Remington Pat. 11-9-37"

c.1935 Celluloid 2 blade $100.00
"Drink Coca-Cola in Bottles" on
opp. side, blade marked "Remington"

c.1935 Pearl w/corkscrew $50.00
Blade Marked "Colonial Prov. R.I."

c.1950-1970 Stainless $20.00 to $30.00
1 blade and nail file, numerous logo
designs & Manufacturers.

c.1930 Boy Scout $85.00
3 diff. shown, Bone & Plastic
handles, diff. shaped shields,
most with blade Marked
"Coca-Cola Bottling Co."

c.1930 Pearl w/corkscrew $100.00
"Pure As Sunlight" on opp. side blade
Marked "Imperial Prov. R.I."

c.1948 Stainless $50.00
2 blade, "The Coca-Cola
Bottling Co." opp. side

c.1940 Pearl, 2 blade $100.00
"Westinghouse" on opp. side,
blade marked "Made by Winchester
Trademark" & "Quickpoint St. Louis"

c.1960.1970 2 blade $10.00
Gold colored plating

Additional Knives can be found on page 212

OPENERS

The majority of the early openers were bought directly from the manufacturer by the bottlers. This accounts for a very large number of styles, types and varieties of openers. We have tried to show a representative assortment here, but with an emphasis on the rarer and unusual. Many of the earlier openers have a small square "Prestolite Key" hole, which served as a wrench to adjust the carbide gas for early automobile headlights (prior to widespread adoption of the battery and generator) this has erroneously been called a "skate key" hole. Some of the most sought after openers are the "Figural" styles shown on this page and page 212. Many openers are imprinted with bottler name and town.   (all opener photos courtesy Thom Thompson, Versailles, Ky.)

"Eagle Head" $100.00
c.1912 to late 1920's
(3 different examples)

"Baseball Player" $150.00
c.1914 to 1920's (very scarce)

"Early Morn" (Nude)

"The Calendar Girl" (Clothed)

"Girl" Opener c.1913 to 1930's $125.00
(scarce) 3 different reverse stampings
shown and the 2 available obverses.

"Saber" or "Sword" $150.00
c.1920 to 1930 (scarce)
(example shown has "Purity is
sealed in a bottle" on opp. side)

Brass with Red and Black Enamel
c.1910 to 1920 $50.00 (value
less with paint worn)

Steel with Enamel $50.00
c.1910 to 1920 (red back-
ground and red with green
background)

Bottle Shaped, Glascock $60.00
c.1930

"Spinner", Fish Shaped $100.00
c.1911 to 1930 ("spin to see who
wins" on back)

"Lion Head" c.1910 to 1930 $100.00
(one example with "Goldelle Ginger Ale"
stamped on back)

"Key Ring" Opener c.1905 to 1915 $35.00
(both sides shown) has cigar box cutter and
nail puller, plus square hole.

"Spinner", Hand Shaped $100.00
c.1915 to 1930, 2 examples shown
("spin to see who pays" on back)

"Handy Pocket Companion" $125.00
c.1905 to 1910, button hook, ruler
& key ring combination, 2 examples
shown.

"Shoe Horn" Opener c.1930 to 1940
$150.00

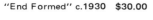

"End Formed" c.1930 $30.00

Cap Lifter, c.1930 $40.00
(opener end bent about 15°
to handle)

"Heavy Duty", c.1930 $40.00
(recent example of this opener
with "Enjoy" . . etc. $3.00)

OPENERS

Most opener styles were available for many years. The dates indicated in most instances are the patent date until probable discontinued use. When this information couldn't be verified, a probable circa date is shown, in most cases an educated guess, based on slogans, logo style, material, weight, etc.

"Improved Perfection" $40.00
c.1930 to 1940 (formed body)

"Cast Iron" c.1900 to 1920 $90.00
(The cast iron openers are some of the first patented openers)

"Perfection" c.1920 to 1930 $20.00
(Raised metal reinforced)

"When Thirsty" c.1908 to 1915 $25.00
Picnic Style, also available with figure 8 key hole and square hole at opener end.

"Ribbed" Opener c.1940 $30.00
Stainless Steel by Dow

"Outing Key Style" $25.00
c.1905 to 1920 (3 examples shown)

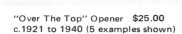

"Over The Top" Opener $25.00
c.1921 to 1940 (5 examples shown)

"Picnic" Opener c.1901 to 1915 $35.00
(Dated 1901)

"Never Slip" Opener $25.00
c.1930 to 1940's (6 examples shown)

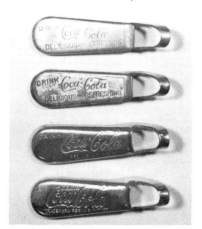

"Formed" Hand Opener $5.00 to $15.00
c.1909 to 1950's many variations, earlier ones marked "Sesco" or "Sealtite" & dated 1909. Later ones marked "Consolidated Cork Corp."

"Walden" Cap Lifter $15.00
(concave handle) c.1950's

"Bottle Stopper" Opener $75.00
c.1919 to 1930 (also example with Glascock Cooler advertising)

"Vaughan's Special" $12.00 to $15.00
c.1920 to 1950's (6 examples shown)
Most common of the pocket openers.
With block letters, In Bottles, or bottlers name, value to $20.00

OPENERS

Many openers are still being produced, some advertising 75th Anniversary celebrations, many in combination with other novelties. Most current openers can be purchased for $1 to $5, depending on quality and supply. There are many foreign openers in the market place, which we have not attempted to show.

"Folding" Can Piercer/Opener $10.00
c.1960 to 1970

"Ribbed" Can Piercer/Opener $20.00
c.1960 to 1970

"Handy Walden" Can Piercer/Opener
c.1963 $50.00 (painted on logo - scarce)

Can Piercer/Opener $1.00 to $3.00
c.1960 to 1980, many variations in
size, length, logo, mfgr., etc.

"Muddler" Opener $175.00
c.1948, heavy brass (scarce)

"Bone Handle" Wire Opener $20.00
c.1930 to 1940

"Plastic Handle" Can Piercer,
Bottle Opener. c.1950 to 1970 $5.00

"Ice Pick" (4 in 1 handy tool) $75.00
c.1912 to 1930

"Ice Pick, Bottle Opener" $60.00
c.1915 to 1940

"Spoon Opener" c.1930 $60.00
(There are many variations of the spoon with opener
handle style available)

"Bottle Cap" Design $50.00
1950 & 1952, 50th Annv. with
presentation box.

"Drink" Wire Opener $3.00
c.1928 to mid 1940's (earlier
variations have "Delicious &
Refreshing" opp. side $15.00

"Have A Coke" Wire Opener $1.00
c.Late 1940's to 1960 (Common)
(Later variations with current
slogans $1.00 each

"Formed Metal"
Wall Mount Opener
c.1948 to 1950 $35.00
Red Enamel logo.

"Bottle Cap" Opener $50.00
c.1950 (With actual bottle cap
attached to wall mount opener)

"Nashville 50th Anniv."
1952 Gold Plated $40.00

Bottle Shaped c.1950
$75.00

"Card Suit Openers" $10.00 Each
c.1970, stainless steel (only sleeves
are marked)

"Syrup Can" Opener c.1940's $25.00

"Never Chip" Wall Opener $40.00
c.1920 to 1950

"Toothed" Wall Opener $75.00
c.1930, The Protector Mfg. Co.

"Wall Mount", Bent Plate Opener $40.00
c.1929 to 1940 (2 examples shown)

OPENERS AND KNIVES

c.1910 to 1930 "Horse Head"
(very scarce opener) $175.00

"Bathing Girl" (clothed) and "Mermaid" (nude)

c.1916 to 1940 "Nifty" combination
bottle opener and corkscrew
(2 varieties shown) $50.00

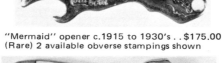

"Mermaid" opener c.1915 to 1930's . . $175.00
(Rare) 2 available obverse stampings shown

c.1920 "Boot" bone handle
opener, pocket knife, "Henry
Sears & Son, 1865, Solingen"
stamped on both blades . $250.00

c.1940 Key shaped pocket knife,
celluloid face. "Kent U.S.A." stamped
on back. "Kent" and "Patent Applied
for" stamped on blade $100.00

c.1920
"Jim Dandy"
combination button
hook, bottle opener, screw
driver, cigar cutter (very scarce)   . . $175.00

c.1920 "Dancer", legs with ballet
slippers & garter $100.00

c.1915 "Legs", bare legs with garter
(with square gas hole) $100.00

c.1910, 2 bladed pocket knife, silver panels,
"Coca-Cola Bottling Co. Germany" and
"D. Peres, Solingen Germany" stamped on
blade $350.00

c.1940, single blade with opener, ebony handle, "Be Smart" and
"Sell Coca-Cola" in window, "Solingen Germany" and "Pat. Pend."
stamped on blade $150.00

c.1932 Wall opener
cast "Hoof shaped"
$35.00

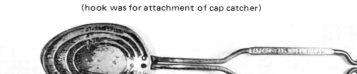

c.1929 thru 1942 Starr "X" Wall mount cast
opener, dated Apr. 1925 . . . $2.00 to $3.00
Mint in original box $8.00

c.1925 Cast wall
opener, corkscrew
and hook. Dated
Apr. 1925 . $60.00

c.1940 Cast wall
opener, chromed,
corkscrew and
hook. . $50.00

c.1950-1960's
Cast wall opener
chromed, cork-
screw . . $20.00

c.1925 "Starr"
Cast wall opener
Dated Apr. 1925
$20.00

(hook was for attachment of cap catcher)

c.1940's to 1980's Starr "X" Wall mount cast
opener. Patent 2,033,088 (issued 1943)
opener only . . . . $1.00 to $2.00
Mint in original box $5.00
(still being made by "Brown Mfg., Co.")

Top c.1930's combination measuring spoon and wire handled cap lifter or opener . . . $75.00
Bottom c.1930's wire handled meat fork $75.00

Similar pieces exist with "Slotted Ladle", "Cake Server", "Pancake
Turner", "Spatula", Etc., most with openers or cap lifters at end of
handle.

1920's with corkscrew and bottle opener . . $25.00

1920's $35.00

1920's-30's with bottle opener $15.00

1930's with bottle opener in box $25.00

1940's-50's in box $20.00

1960's $5.00

1920's Ice Tongs $150.00

1960's $5.00

1950's Helena, Ark. $8.00

1920's Fly Swatter
showing both sides $50.00

1960's Tarboro, N.C. (plastic) $5.00

MISCELLANEOUS

c.1950's Hohner Harmonica (miniature) Key Ring, in leather case (German) $75.00

"Refresh Yourself"

"Our Only Competitor" (stamped cow)

Bottled Coca-Cola Roddy Mfg., Co.

c.1930 Bell (stamped metal) (front and back same) 3¼'' high $175.00

c.1920 Bell (stamped metal), front & back shown, brass plated steel, 3¼'' high $225.00

c.1930 Brass equipment tag or key tag, 2¾'' . . . $35.00

c.1920's Bell (enameled printing, not stamped) 2¼'' high, front and back shown $200.00

c.1950's Key Ring Nashville, TN. . . $25.00

c.1930 Routeman's Pin (Indianapolis, bottling co.) 2½'' brass $75.00

c.1910 Uniform Button ¾'' $45.00

c.1920 Security Guards Badge Coca-Cola Bottling Co., Ind., Chromed 2½'' $100.00

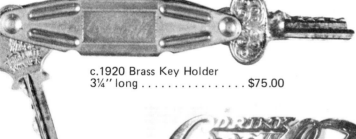

c.1920 Brass Key Holder 3¼'' long $75.00

c.1920 Hat Pin, Chromed 4'' . . . $100.00

c.1950's 50th Anniversary Key Chain $8.00

c.1959 Car Key $10.00

c.1930's "Cloisonne" Hat Pin, 1 1/8''X 2'' . . $125.00

MISCELLANEOUS

c.1920 Thimble $25.00
(Many varieties of these
aluminum thimbles
exist, both red and blue
enamel inlay).

c.1920's Celluloid Cufflinks
pair of red $50.00
pair of blue $75.00

c.1920's Salt and Pepper Shakers,
aluminum with enamel inlay.
pair of shakers $275.00
in original box $300.00

c.1912 Lapel Pin
$125.00
(Whithead and Hoag)

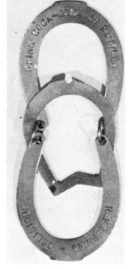

c.1920's Puzzle (metal)
$150.00

c.1920's cardboard "Cat" pocket mirror
2½" X 2½" Rare $300.00

The Family That Prays Together Stays Together

c.1950's metal switch plate cover
with thermometer. $75.00
(bottler item)

c.1960's sterling silver bottle
earrings $30.00

c.1913-1915 Door Knobs, 2 different sizes available,
in both brass and steel . . . . $250.00 Each
(Used in the Coca-Cola buildings in K.C., Mo., and
Baltimore, Md., built by Asa Candler in 1913 & 1915.)

c.1960 Perfume Bottle
sterling silver case,
with applied sterling
bottle $200.00

c.1950 Bottle Stopper
enameled plaster Sprite
Boy head with cork
neck $150.00

c.1950 Garment Hanger
(plastic) in orig. package
$35.00

c.1920's Compact (celluloid) with powder puff
2¼", "Parisian Nov. Co., Chicago" . . $250.00

1940's Sewing Kits, U.S. Marines, U.S. Army,
(not shown U.S. Navy & Coast Guard) . . $25.00 Each

c.1960's Money Clip
Knife $20.00

c.1960's Money Clip
Knife $20.00

PINBACK BUTTONS

Late 1930's . . . $30.00

1950's . . . $8.00

1977 . . . $4.00

1976 . . . $3.00

1960's . . . $5.00

1960's . . . $8.00

1970's . . . $2.00

1970's . . . $2.00

1980's . . . $2.00

1980's . . . $2.00

1960's . . . $6.00

1980's . . . $3.00

1970's . . . $3.00

1980's . . . $2.00

1980's . . . $3.00

1970's Sprite . . . $2.00

1950's $10.00

1950's . $5.00 Ea.

1977 . . . $2.00

1980's . . $2.00

1970's . . . $2.00

1980's . . . $1.00

1970's . . . $2.00

1980's . . . $2.00

1970's $3.00

1980's . . . $3.00

1983 . . . $2.00

1981 . . . $2.00

1980's . . . $4.00

1976 . . . $3.00

WALLETS AND CHANGE PURSES

c.1912 Change Purse $85.00

c.1910 Change Purse $75.00

c.1908 . . . . $85.00

c.1907 . . . . $65.00

c.1907 . . $50.00

c.1920's . . $25.00

1918 w/Calendar
$50.00

c.1920's with Envelope . . $150.00

1950's $10.00

1928 Billfold $20.00

c.1920's with embossed
1916 bottle . . . $20.00

1920's . . $20.00

1950's . $10.00

1950's w/Box
$12.00

NOTE: Wallets and Change Purses are difficult to date.
In most cases, the dates are just good estimates.

I have seen many different examples of wallets and
change purses. This is just a small sampling of the
many different types that have been given away by
The Coca-Cola Company over the years.

STRAWS

1960's . . . $15.00

Early 1940's . . . $45.00

1940's $50.00

Late 1940's to 1950's
$45.00

c.1939 . . $50.00

1960's $15.00

NOTE: These prices reflect full or
near full boxes of straws. Empty
boxes would be worth considerably
less.

PENCILS AND PENCIL HOLDERS

1960's Ceramic Pencil Holder $150.00

NOTE: A reproduction of this pencil holder was produced in the 1980's to
commemorate the 75th Anniversary of the New York Bottling Co., it is so
marked and worth approximately $50.00

c.1940's through 1960's Mechanical Pencil . . $15.00 with box . $25.00
NOTE: There are many variations of this pencil, many bottlers had their
name imprinted on the pencils they gave out.

Early 1940's 12 Pack (plastic ferrules
used during WWII $25.00
Single Pencil $2.00

1938 through the 40's and 50's
(except WWII) $20.00
Single Pencil $1.00

1960's 12 Pack $15.00
Single Pencil $1.00

1970's 12 Pack $3.00
Single Pencil 25

1970's 12 Pack $3.00
Single Pencil 25

MATCHBOOKS AND MATCH HOLDERS

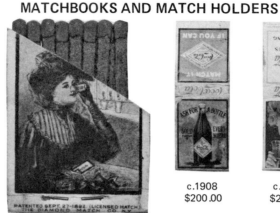

1922 . . . . . $50.00

c.1908
$200.00

c.1912
$200.00

c.1907 Leather
Matchbook Holder
$125.00

1910 Match Safe
$450.00

1908 . . Rare . . $300.00

c.1910 Matchbook Holder . $100.00

c.1914 . . $200.00

SAME BACK

c.1913 . . $200.00

1912 . . . . . $250.00

| 1930's | 1930's | 1936 | 1936 | 1940's | 1952 | 1940's | 1950's |
| $10.00 | $5.00 | $5.00 | $6.00 | $5.00 | $4.00 | $3.00 | $6.00 |

| 1950's | 1959 | 1950's | 1963 | 1963 | 1964 | 1963 | 1960's |
| $1.00 | $2.00 | $3.00 | $2.00 | $2.00 | $1.00 | $1.00 | $2.00 |

| 1958 . .$6.00 | 1964 | 1959 | 1963 | 1959 | 1959 | 1970's | 1970's |
| | $4.00 | $2.00 | $2.00 | $2.00 | $2.00 | .50 | .50 |

ASH TRAYS, LIGHTERS, ETC.

c.1940's "Match Holder Ash Tray"
$325.00

1936 "50th Anniversary"
Frosted Glass Cigarette Box . . . $275.00

c.1950's Ruby Glass
Ash Tray Set $175.00

c.1959 Metal Matchbook
Holder (full) $50.00

1939 Porcelain
Match Striker . . $125.00
(Canada)

c.1950's . . $10.00

Shelbyville, Ind.
New Plant Ash Tray . $40.00

1963 Musical
Lighter . . $50.00

1964 . $6.00

1950's Aluminum
$5.00

1960's Aluminum . $5.00

1950's . . $8.00

1960 Mini Can
Lighter . $8.00

1960's
Lighter . $8.00

c.1940's
Glass . . $10.00

1970's Glass . $2.00

1969
Aluminum . .$5.00

1960 Mini
Lighter . $15.00

1950's
Lighter. $10.00

ASHTRAYS AND PAPERWEIGHTS

1950's with bottle lighter . . $75.00
Bottle lighter only $5.00

Late 1920's $50.00

1950's $45.00

1960's Mexico . $5.00

1950's . . . $6.00

1970's Mexico . . $3.00

1966 "World Press Institute Dinner" Showing Coke caps from around the world $60.00

1974 . . . . $6.00

1958 Atlanta $35.00

1970's $3.00

Lucite Paperweight with around the world bottle caps $30.00

1974 Lucite Paperweight . . $8.00

1970's . . $5.00

1970's Mexico . . $3.00

COASTERS

1940's $8.00

1940's Rubber Coasters
Complete set in envelope $15.00
Individual coasters $2.00

1950's $3.00

1950's . . . $5.00

1939 . . . . $5.00

1940's . . . . $5.00 Each

1960's . . . $3.00

1950's $5.00

c.1950 . . . $3.00

1950's . . . $3.00

1950's . . . $2.00

1960's . . . $2.00

1960's $2.00

1970's . . . $1.00

1970's foreign . . . . . . $2.00 Each

1970's . . $1.00

1970's . . . $1.00

1970's . . . $1.00

1950's Metal $10.00

1960's Metal
Sales Award
$5.00

1960's Aluminum
$3.00

1950's foreign $5.00

COASTERS

1950's German . . . . . . $5.00 Each

1970's - 80's
Set of ceramic coasters in wood base
$10.00

1980's 75th Anniversary coaster
$2.00

1980's Set of 6 coasters
"History of Coca-Cola"
Each $2.00
Set of 6 . . . . . $20.00

1937 Nazi Germany coaster, showing both sides . . . . Rare $125.00

1950's Canadian . . . . $5.00 Each

1950's Coaster/Ash Tray (foil)
Russellville, Ky. $6.00

1950's Foil coasters . . . . $3.00 Each

1966 Set of 8 plastic coasters (in box)
Fountain Sales Dept., Sales Meeting
$20.00

1980's Jumbo coaster . . $3.00

STAMP HOLDERS AND NOTE PADS

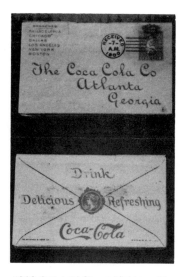

1902 Celluloid Postage Stamp Carrier, 1½''X 2½'' . . . $300.00

1910 Celluloid Stamp Holder 1¾''X 2'',with pullout calendar and tissue stamp pages. $300.00

1900 Celluloid Stamp Holder with Calendar 1½''X 2½'' $300.00

1902 Celluloid Note Pad, 2½''X 5'' $350.00

1903 Celluloid Note Pad, 2½''X 5'' $350.00

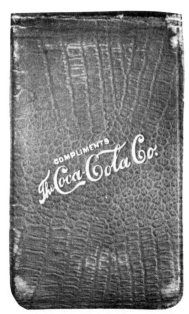

1903 Note Book 2¾''X 5¾'', brown leather with gold embossing . . . . . $200.00 (This book also put out in 1904, 1905 and 1906, listing all syrup sales.

1905 Note Book, 2¾''X 4½'' . . $150.00

-224-

MENUS

1904 4 1/8'' X 6½'' Lillian Nordica . . . $400.00

1903 4 1/8''X 6 1/8'' Hilda Clark $375.00

1902 4 1/8''X 6 1/8''. . . . $400.00

NOTE: The back of these menus are very interesting, when framing make sure the back is displayed.

Back of Menus

1901 Hilda Clark (shown open 11¾''X 4'') $575.00

BOOKMARKS

1903 2''X 6'' . . . . $275.00   1904 2''X 6'' . . . . $200.00   1905 2¼''X 5¼'' $375.00

1900 2''X 2¼'' Celluloid, 2 different examples . . . . . $400.00 Each   1898 2''X 2¼'' Celluloid . . $450.00

c.1906 1 1/2 ''X 3 1/8 '' ''OWL'' Celluloid . . $500.00

c.1897   2 3/8 ''X 2 3/4 '' Celluloid
Rare $650.00

1899 2''X 2¼'' Celluloid . . $450.00

 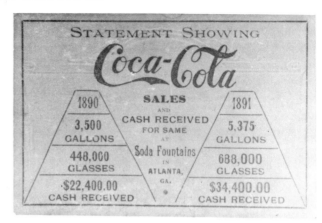

1892, 3½" X 5¼", Trade Card, shows Machinery Hall of the upcoming 1893 World's Columbian Exposition, Chicago, Ill., back shows 1890 and 1891 fountain sales (photo courtesy: Thom Thompson) ......Rare $1,000.00

1902 Trade Card 4 1/8 "x 6 1/8" Rare ..... $425.00   1901 Trade Card 2 1/4" X 3 7/8" Rare .. $475.00

c.1898-1901 U.S. Proprietary Revenue
Stamp with Coca-Cola cancellation . $150.00

c.1908 Business Card 2"x 3½" .. $25.00

1898 Track Field Day Program (paper folder) with "Imperial Cafe" of Atlanta, and "Coco-Cola" (note misspelling)
advertising on back $250.00

POSTCARDS

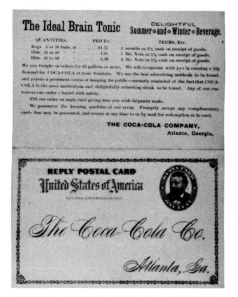

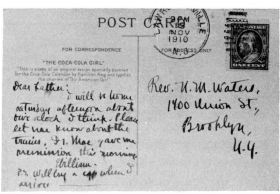

1893 Double Postal Card . . . $600.00
NOTE: Pieces this early are very Rare.
Photo Courtesy: Thom Thompson

1910 "The Coca-Cola Girl"
Hamilton King Artwork $375.00

1911 "Motor Girl"
(Formally called the "Duster Girl") . . $400.00

NOTE: Although an unused postcard in flawless condition would be very desirable, I personally prefer a used "postmarked" card, which I find so much more interesting.

c.1898 . . . . $300.00

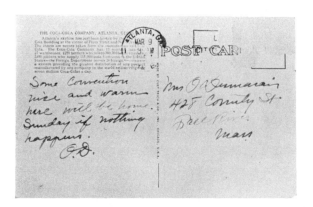

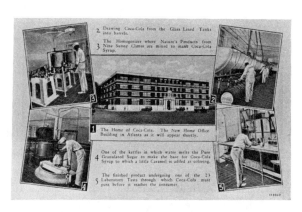

c.1920's "The Home of Coca-Cola" in Atlanta $85.00

POSTCARDS

c.1906 Soda Fountain, Photo Card $100.00

NOTE: Pre-1920 Soda Fountain cards showing Coke advertising especially photo cards are always very desirable.

1910 "Reminder" Card $75.00

1936 "Free Calendar" Postcard $25.00

1912 Brown's Pharmacy, Ozark, Al. . . . $40.00

1930's Atlantic, Ia. Bottling Plant $35.00

30 Caliber Machine Gun, Water Cooled

50 Caliber Machine Gun Trainer

1940's "Cartoon"
Post Card Sets
(4 cards to a set)

5 different sets shown

Complete set
in wrapper . . . $50.00

Individual cards . . $3.00 Each

1944 Army Exibit Post Card
2 different fronts shown, same back . . $10.00 Each

POSTCARDS

International Truck Post Card $8.00

1906 and 1909 Candler Building Atlanta, Ga.
$10.00 Each

1930's Richfield Oil . . . $8.00

1930's Weldmech Truck . $15.00

Early 1900's
Candler Building
Atlanta, Ga. . $10.00

1916 Coca-Cola
Building KC, Mo.
$8.00

1920's Coca-Cola Building
Baltimore, MD . . . $25.00

1930's Coca-Cola Bottling Co.
Little Rock, AK . . . $15.00

c.1907 . . . . . $20.00

c.1907 Atlantic City $8.00

1940's Bakersfield, Ca. $4.00

Early 20's Ad Agency
Post Card $25.00

1940's Christmas "May We Suggest" Post Card
2 different versions . . . . $4.00 Each

1920's Brown Mfg., Co.
Order Post Card . . . $20.00

1940's Free Bottle
Opener . . $10.00

1968 Coke Pavilion
Worlds Fair . . $3.00

1964 Coke Pavilion
Worlds Fair . . . $3.00

1970's (Bobby Allison) Coke Race Car
$5.00 Each

FOLDING CARDS

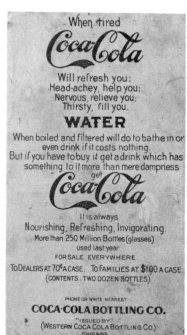

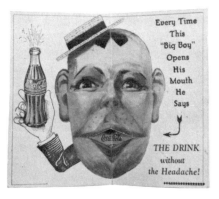

c.1907 Folding Trade Card
Showing Open, Closed and Reverse $475.00

c.1920's Mechanical Folding
Card $350.00

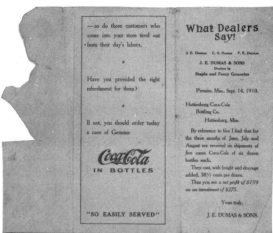

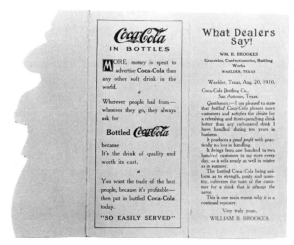

c.1910 Folding Advertising Cards. (These cards were sent out on a monthly basis to prospective dealers of Coca-Cola) . $300.00 Each

COUPONS

1901 Hilda Clark
1 5/8''X 3 3/8'' $300.00

c.1908 (purple)
1 5/8''X 3 3/8'' $125.00

Pre-1900 Seth W. Fowle & Sons
1 1/2''X 3 3/8'' $150.00

1901 Hilda Clark
1 5/8''X 3 3/8'' different back . . $300.00

c.1908 (red and green)
1 5/8''X 3 3/8'' $200.00

Pre-1900 "The Coca-Cola Company"
1 1/2''X 3 3/8'' $150.00

NOTE: These early coupons were called "Complimentary Tickets" by The Coca-Cola Company.

1905 "Lillian Nordica" magazine ad with coupon, placed in 9 different magazines in the summer of 1905. 6½''X 9¾'' .... $90.00 (back similar to that at right)

1905 "Lillian Nordica" Ad Card with coupon, 3¾''X 7'' (front and back shown) .... $350.00 Rare when found complete, coupon Must be attached to warrant this price.

1909, 1910, 1911 Calendar $325.00 A large quantity of these "Ad Cards" (shown at left) were converted to a small size calendar by "Wolf & Co." in the above years. The coupon was removed and a metal grommet added for hanging. This calendar is old and original. Why this art work was used again, so many years after it's first 1905 usage is really not known. This calendar was pictured in the April 1949 Coca-Cola Bottler magazine, which disputes speculation by some that this was a piece fabricated in the 1970's.

COUPONS

c.1930's 1½"X 2¾" .. $5.00
(box carton on back)

c.1930 2"X 2½" .. $4.00

c.1903 (purple and green)
1 5/8"X 3 3/8" $200.00

Pre-1900 "The Coca-Cola Company"
1½"X 3 3/8" $150.00

GOOD FOR 5 CENTS

c.1920's 1 1/8"X 2"
$5.00

c.1906 2¾"X 5 1/8" .. $50.00

THIS TICKET AND ONE
Coca-Cola
BOTTLE
5 cts.

c.1930 2½"X 4"
$5.00

1934 2"X 4" .. $15.00

Late 1920's 2 1/8"X 3½" .. $10.00

1950's 2 7/8"X 4" . $2.00

c.1950 2 3/8"X 4 3/8" .. $5.00

c.1927 "Soda Jerk"
2¼"X 4" ... $35.00
(front and back shown)

Late 1920's Coupon Book
2"X 5" $10.00

c.1929 2 3/8"X 3 5/8" ... $25.00

1939 2 3/8"X 4 3/8" .. $5.00

c.1939 2½"X 4" .. $5.00

1930's Bottle Shaped
1¾"X 6" $3.00

Late 1920's "Thomas Coupon"
2"X 2¾" $2.00

Late 1920's
3 Coupons in envelope.. $25.00
Individual Coupons .. $3.00 Each
(2½"X 3½")

COUPONS

Below are 14 different examples of "Complimentary" 6 bottle coupon cards. They were used during the late 30's. Some are quite common and range in price from $5.00 to about $15.00.

Early 1950's . . . $5.00

BLOTTERS

Shown on the following pages is the most complete and accurately dated collection of Coca-Cola blotters ever illustrated, my special thanks to Thom Thompson of Versailles, Ky. for his extensive research and collaboration on this section. Blotters from 1904 through 1923 were issued either advertising "Bottled"(B) Sales or Advertising "Fountain"(F) Sales. After c.1923 they all advertised bottled sales.

c.1904 (F) $75.00
"Edwards Deutsch & Heitmann, Chicago"

C.1904 (F) $325.00
"Atlanta Litho & Printing, Co."

c.1904 (B) $450.00   c.1904 (B) $325.00   c.1904 (B) $325.00
"Atlanta Litho &   "Edwards Deutsch &   (No Litho Co.)
Print, Co."   Heitmann, Chicago"

C.1905 (B) $125.00

c.1906 (B) $100.00

c.1906 (F) $100.00   1909 (B) $150.00   C.1909 (F) $100.00

1911 (B) $450.00
Blue & Pink Backs.
"Motor Girl"
(previously called
"Duster Girl")

 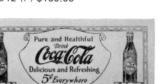 

1910 (B) $250.00   c.1912 (F) $100.00   c.1913 (F) $25.00

C.1913 (B) $25.00   c.1915 (B) $60.00   c.1915 (F) $150.00

c.1916 (B) $20.00   c.1920 (F) $85.00   c.1920 (B) $30.00

c.1923 (B) $20.00   c.1923 (F) $200.00   c.1924 (B) $200.00

c.1926 (B) $10.00   c.1915 "Chewing Gum" $750.00   c.1916 "Chewing Gum" $500.00

BLOTTERS

1927 . . . $35.00

1928 . . . $45.00

1929 . . . $150.00

1929 . . . $75.00

1929 . . $100.00

1929 . . $75.00

1930 . . . $35.00

1930 . . . $50.00

1930 . . . $100.00

1930 . . . $75.00

1931 . . . $125.00

1931 . . . $125.00

1931 . . $100.00

1931 . . . $75.00

1932-33 . . . $50.00

1932-33 . . . $75.00

1932-33 . . . $125.00

1932-33 . . . $100.00

1934 . . . $75.00

1934 . . . $75.00

1934 . . . $75.00

1934 . . . $75.00

1935(dated &undated) $35.00

1935(dated & undated) $15.00

1935(dated & undated) $15.00

1935(dated & undated) $20.00

1936 . . . $40.00

1937 . . . $15.00

1938 . . . $10.00

1939 . . . $10.00

1940 . . . $40.00

1941(TM in tail & w/o) $5.00

1942 . . . $2.00

1942 . . . $3.00

1944 . . . $3.00

1947 . . . $3.00

1951 . . . $2.00

1952 . . . $40.00

1953 . . . $2.00

1956 . . . $2.00

1957 . . . $3.00

1960 . . . $2.00

1942 . . . $5.00

1942 . . . $5.00

c.1950 . . $5.00

BLOTTERS

The following are miscellaneous blotters not used by "The Coca-Cola Co.", and stock blotters used by individual bottlers as well as pencil box blotters.

c.1911 "WESTERN" $100.00

1931 . . . $75.00

1905 "PALATKA" $200.00

1944 Dispensers . . . $75.00
(Coca-Cola Machine on right)

c.1907 . . $100.00

1906 "WESTERN" $200.00
(Shown trimmed down)

1935 or 1937 . . . $5.00

1935 or 1937 . . . $5.00
Pencil Box Blotters
Issued by The Coca-Cola Co.

── The following are Foreign Blotters. ──

c.1904 CUBA . . . $200.00

c.1909 CUBA . . . $200.00

c.1935 GERMAN . . . $100.00

c.1935 . $100.00
CANADA

1942 MEXICAN. . $5.00

1947 "Export Corp" . . . $60.00

1938 CANADA . . . $30.00

1939 CANADA . . $40.00

c.1947 BELGIUM . . $60.00

1940 CANADA(Fr.) . . $40.00

1945 CANADA . . . $50.00

1946 CANADA . . $20.00

1947 CANADA . . $30.00

1948 CANADA . . $15.00

1949 CANADA . . $30.00

1950 CANADA . . $20.00

1951 CANADA(Eng.) . . $30.00

1951 CANADA(Fr.) . . $30.00

1954 . . . $15.00
CANADA (Fr.)

1954 . . . $15.00
CANADA(Eng.)

1952 CANADA . . $30.00

1953 CANADA . . $20.00

1955 CANADA . . $20.00

Almost all Canadian blotters have been printed in both French and English.
Some of these variations are shown above.
*NOTE: There have been times when a good blotter has turned up in quantity. If and when
this happens, a $100.00 blotter could become a $20.00 blotter.*

-237-

PLAYING CARDS

| 1909 . . $900.00 | 1915 . . $600.00 | 1928 . . $225.00 | 1937 . . $100.00 | 1938 . . $75.00 | 1939 . . $100.00 | 1939 . . $100.00 |

| 1939 . . $175.00 | 1943 . . $45.00 | 1943 . . $45.00 | 1943 . . $45.00 | 1943 . . $45.00 | 1943 . . $85.00 | 1943 . . $75.00 |

| 1951 . . $45.00 | 1951 . . $45.00 | 1956 . . $40.00 | 1956 . . $40.00 | 1958 . . $40.00 | 1958 . . $40.00 | 1959 . . $35.00 |

| 1959 . . $35.00 | 1960 . . $35.00 | 1960 . . $40.00 | 1961 . . $30.00 | 1961 . . $30.00 | 1963 . . $35.00 | 1963 . . $30.00 |

| 1963 . . $30.00 | 1963 . . $30.00 | 1971 Boy Scouts Jamboree . $65.00 | 1971 . . $6.00 | 1971 . . $6.00 | 1971 Mexico $10.00 |

| 1974 . . . $5.00 | 1976 . . . $5.00 | 1976 . . . $5.00 | 1970's ''Bucks'' . . . . $30.00 |

NOTE: The prices shown here are for full decks in original box, in average condition. Decks that are mint or sealed in original box would be worth more, and decks that are worn or without box are worth less. Always consider the condition of the deck when determining value.

PLAYING CARDS, BRIDGE, ETC.

1950 NAPL Convention
Bridge set $85.00

1950's Bridge tally card . . $8.00

1950's Bridge tally cards . . $8.00 Each

1960's Bridge set (case) . . $10.00

1938 12"X 18" cardboard sign . . $25.00

1940's Bridge score pad
and tally card . .$8.00 set

BRIDGE
SCORE PAD

1980's Bridge score
pad $2.00

1943 Score pad . . $6.00

1930's - 40's Score pad
(Canada) $3.00

1950's Bridge Digest
booklet $8.00

1950's Bridge tally card . . $8.00

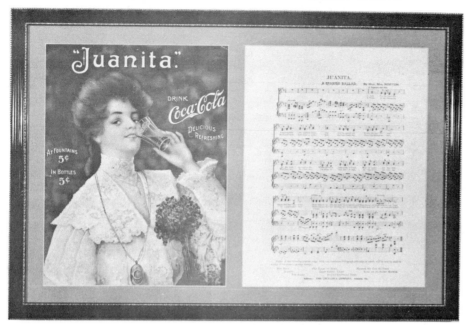

1906 "Juanita" $750.00

Additional titles of
1906 "Juanita" sheet music
not shown.

- Ben Bolt
- My Old Kentucky Home
- Rock Me To Sleep Mother
- Old Folks At Home
- Lead Kindly Light
- Nearer, My God To Thee

NOTE:
*This art work has been
dubbed "Juanita" by
collectors. For that
reason, I believe the
sheet actually titled
"Juanita" is more
desirable and in turn
worth more than
other titles.*

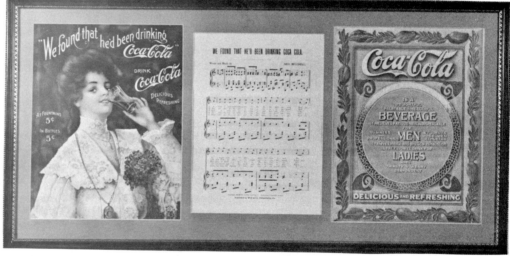

1906 "We Found That He'd Been Drinking Coca-Cola" $500.00

1906 "The Palms" $500.00

1906 "My Coca-Cola Bride" $500.00

SHEET MUSIC

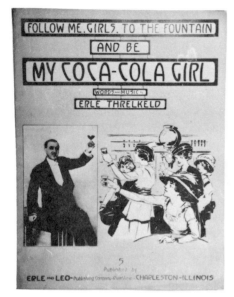

1915 "Follow me girls to the fountain and be my Coca-Cola girl"
10¾"X 13¾" (amusing compliments to Coca-Cola Co., by author), Rare . . $300.00

1942 "Theme Song" for the
Coca-Cola Co., 9"X 12" . . $35.00

1927 "The Coca-Cola Girl" 9½"X 12½" $200.00
(This piece of sheet music is not too difficult to find, therefore it must be Mint to warrant this price.)

1944 "Rum and Coca-Cola"
(French printed version)
10½"X 13" $35.00

1913 "My Coco-Cola Belle", pictures
Fannie Brice, 10½"X 13½" $300.00
(misspelled "Coco-Cola" on cover, inside title
and lyrics spelled "Coca-Cola")

SHEET MUSIC

c.1912 "When The Do-Do Bird Is Singing
In The Coca-Cola Tree" $225.00

1941 "We Stand United" $15.00

1940's "Rum & Coca-Cola"
Jeri Sullavan . . . $20.00

1940's "Rum & Coca-Cola"
The Andrew Sisters . . . $15.00

1941 "Favorite American Songs"
Music Book $15.00

1970's "Look Up America" . . $5.00

1972 "Country Sunshine"
$3.00

1970's "I'd Like To Buy
The World A Coke" . . . $3.00

RECORDS

1950's Eddie Fisher 78 Record
with original sleeve $25.00

1960's Salesman's Training Record
33 1/3 . . . . . $6.00

1940's Salesman's Training Record
33 1/3 . . . . . $10.00

1950's Eddie Fisher Cardboard Poster
(record offer) $50.00
45 Record only $5.00

1960's "Swing The Jingle"
45 Record . $15.00 with sleeve

1970's "It's The Real Thing"
45 Record . . . $2.00

RECORDS

1953-1957 Eddie Fisher
45 RPM Record & Sleeve $10.00

1968 "Camelot", Los Angeles,
Bottling Co., 45RPM . . . $3.00

1965 "Sue Thompson Swings The
Jingle", 33 1/3 RPM Record &
Sleeve (Canada) $15.00

1963 "Here and Now"
songs from 1963 con-
vention, with folder
insert, 45RPM . . $10.00

Back of Eddie Fisher Sleeve

Eddie Fisher
Bottle Hanger,
Record Offer
for 25c . . $10.00

1962 "Anita Bryant Refreshing
New Feeling" Radio Spots,
33 1/3 RPM $15.00

1958 "Theme Music" 45 RPM
Record and Sleeve . . . $20.00

c.1950 Sleeve only for 45 RPM
"Rum and Coca-Cola"
(Foreign) $5.00

1970's "I'd like to teach the world
to sing", 45 RPM Record & Sleeve
(Canada) $15.00

1965 "Petula Clark Swings The
Jingle", Radio Spots, 33 1/3 RPM
Record $15.00

1950's "Rum and Coca-Cola"
Andrew Sisters, 45 RPM . $10.00

1967 "Trini Lopez" 45 RPM
Record & Sleeve, advertising
"Fresca" $10.00

c.1950 "Learn to Dance at Home",
by Andy Capps, 45 RPM . . $5.00

1960's Cardboard Sleeve with
Coca-Cola advertising, contained
Top Hit 45 RPM (Canada) . . $5.00

-244-

RECORDS

Late 1940's
Early 1950's
Salesman's Training Records 33 1/3 . . . . . . $10.00 Each

1970's Original Radio Broadcast Albums
$12.00 Each

1982 Penn State
"Coke Is It"
45 Record . . $10.00

1960's "12 Top Hits"
Album $25.00

1960's - 1970's "Radio Spots" Tape
$10.00 Each

1951 Tony Bennett
45 Record with sleeve
$10.00

FANS

1930's . . . . $20.00 Each
(2 different examples)

1890's 7'' X 12¼'' Rare . . . $3,000.00

1920's $100.00

c.1911 (Showing front and 2 different backs) . . . . . . $125.00 Each

1930's $30.00

1950's (Ft. Myers, Fla.) $25.00

1930's (St. Louis, Mo.) $30.00

FANS

c.1900 . . . . $125.00   c.1900 . . . . $125.00

1926 Heavy Cardboard
(one piece) Rare $200.00
This Fan was actually part of a
display piece.

c. 1950's Wicker $20.00

c. 1930's $40.00

c. 1950's $35.00

c. 1920's $25.00

1940's - 50's $6.00

FANS

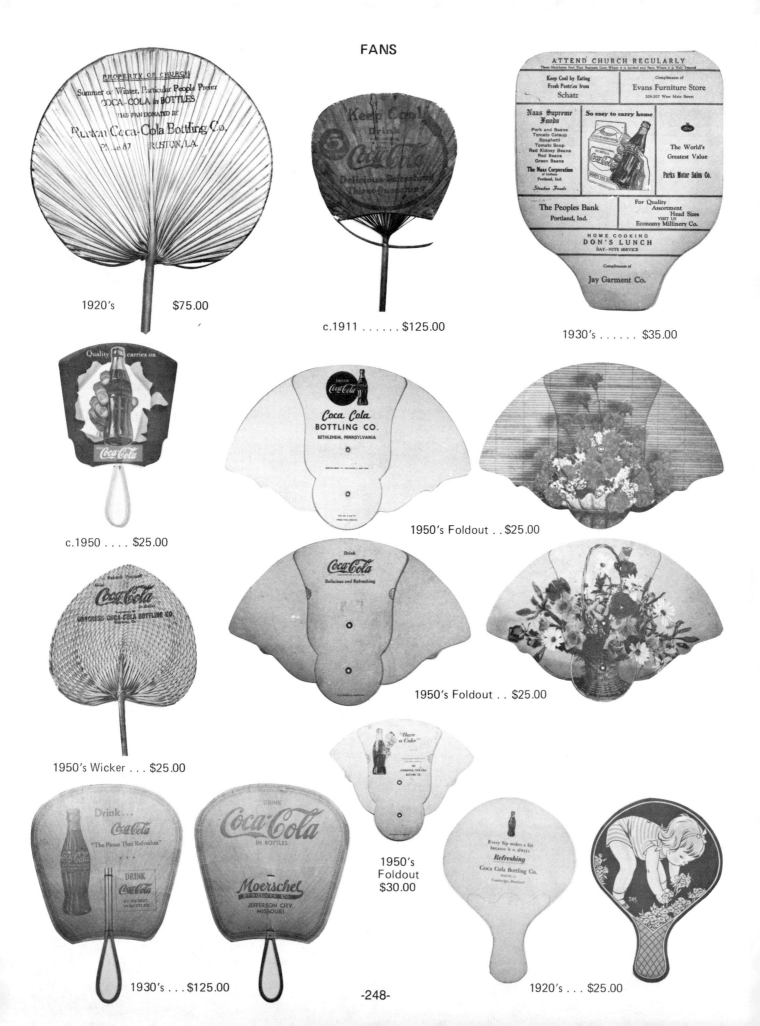

1920's $75.00

c.1911 . . . . . $125.00

ATTEND CHURCH REGULARLY

1930's $35.00

c.1950 . . . . $25.00

1950's Foldout . . $25.00

1950's Wicker . . . $25.00

1950's Foldout . . $25.00

1950's Foldout $30.00

1930's . . . $125.00

-248-

1920's . . . $25.00

NAPKINS

NOTE: The printing quality on many of these napkins is certainly not a work of art, but early ones are rare and all are very collectible.

Pre-1900 RARE $475.00

c.1911
$50.00

1912 . . . . $75.00

1960's $3.00

1930's $20.00

1950's $5.00

Early 1900's $50.00

c.1911 . . . . $30.00

PHOTOS AND CATALOG SHEETS

Photo prices listed below are for original photos, reprints have little if any value.

1907 5"X7"
Washington, D.C. . . . $65.00

Early Horse Drawn
Delivery Wagon
Norton, Va. . . . $85.00

1908 Coca-Cola
Delivery Truck
8"X10" . . . $100.00

Early Salesman's
Horse Drawn Wagon
St. Louis, Mo. 5"X7" . . . $65.00

1929 Standard Painting System Chart
Showing Paint Colors by Sherwin Williams Co. $200.00

1940's Truck
Catalog Sheet . . $15.00

Late 30's
Drug Store Photo
8"X10" . . . $10.00

1938 Truck Photo
8"X10" $20.00

1940's Truck
Catalog Sheet . . . $15.00

Late 30's 8"X10" . . $10.00

1920's Delivery Truck
8"X10" . . . $30.00

PHOTOS 8"X 10" Originals Only (reprints have very little value)

Ireland's Drug Store
Portland, Or. . . . $20.00

1923 McAlpine Hotel, NY . . $35.00

1935 Rochester, NY
Display $25.00

1925 Ohio Food Show
Toledo, OH . . . $30.00

1923 Walgreen Drug Store
Chicago. $45.00

1930 Wisconsin Food Show . . $25.00

The Empire Luncheonette
Denver, Co. $20.00

1923 Moberly Ice Cream Co.
Mo. $50.00

1922 Mother Goose Shop
St. Louis, Mo. $35.00

1924 Food Show
Albany, NY . . . $30.00

1920's Billboard
Flint, Mich. . . $20.00

1923 Liggetts N.Y.C. . . $35.00

1920's Santa Display . . $30.00

1923 Wilder Drug Store
Boston, Ma. . . . $35.00

1924 Pure Food Show
Albany, NY . . . $30.00

LETTERHEAD

1906 Atlanta, Ga. . . . $35.00

1919 Letter, envelope, and newspaper stock listing, showing Coca-Cola stock. Handwritten by Howard Candler $125.00

1912 Letter and envelope handwritten and signed by Howard Candler . . $100.00

1889 Letter and envelope from "Asa G. Candler & Co." Atlanta, Ga. $175.00

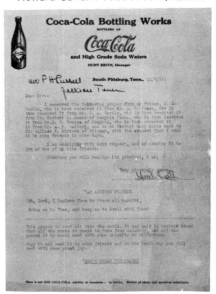

1916 So. Pittsburg, Tenn. . . $8.00

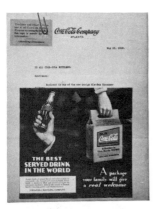

1929 Letter and color folder showing new 6 bottle carrier $35.00

1924 Asa G. Candler letter and envelope handwritten . . $85.00

1915 Letter and envelope from Howard Candler handwritten and signed . . $75.00

LETTERHEAD

1903 Macon Ga. . . . $10.00

c.1910 Waycross Ga. . . . $8.00

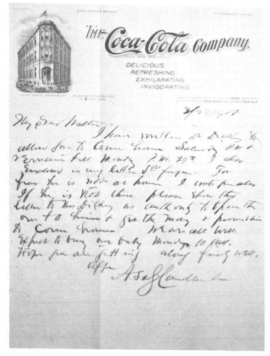

1916 Brunswick Ga. . . . $8.00

1905 Letter and Envelope
from Asa Candler to his son Walter . . . $175.00

1923 Cuthbert Ga. . . . $8.00

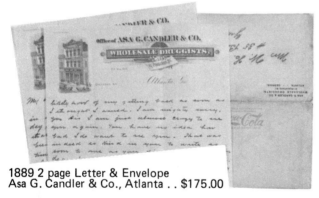

1889 2 page Letter & Envelope
Asa G. Candler & Co., Atlanta . . $175.00

1915 Valdosta Ga. . . . $8.00

1918 Douglas Ga. . . . $5.00

Early 1900's Indianapolis, Ind.
2 page Letter & Envelope . . $125.00

NOTE: Many of these letterheads were used
for years after the bottle change.

-253-

LETTERHEAD

NOTE: An interesting hand signed letter, by company executives or the pioneers of the Coca-Cola business, would certainly increase the value of any letterhead.

1908 . . . . $75.00

1906 . . . . $50.00

1903 . . . . $50.00

1909 . . . . $25.00

1911 . . . . $35.00

c.1912 . . . . $20.00

1909 . . . . $40.00

1903 . . . . $30.00

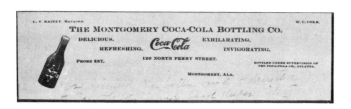

c.1911 . . . . $20.00

1931 . . . . $10.00

INVOICES AND RECEIPTS

1888 Invoice   Asa G. Candler & Co. . . $50.00

1888 Receipt   Asa G. Candler & Co.

Signed by
Asa G. Candler
$175.00

Early 1900's Receipt Paducah, Ky. . . $10.00

1902
Invoice
Atlanta, Ga.
$50.00

1905 Invoice Atlanta, Ga. . . . $50.00

1909 Invoice Atlanta, Ga. . . . $50.00

1903
Invoice
Atlanta, Ga.
$50.00

1900 Invoice Atlanta, Ga. . . . $50.00

1908 Invoice Macon, Ga. . . . $30.00

1916 Invoice Florida Coca-Cola . . . $15.00

ENVELOPES

NOTE: Those envelopes with postmarks and stamps (generally called "Covers") are more desirable.
Some would command a higher value because of the rarity of a stamp.

1897 Boston $30.00

1898 Coca-Cola Company . . . $50.00

1898 Complimentary Ticket
Envelope $35.00

1904 Richmond, Va. . . . $20.00

1905 The Coca-Cola Co. . . . $25.00

1913 Sanford, N.C. . . . $25.00
(Hires Rootbeer printing on flap)

Early 1900's Waycross, Georgia (printed on both sides) $50.00

1918 The Coca-Cola Company . . $15.00

1923 Zanesville, Ohio . . . $15.00

1912 Baltimore, Md. . . . $20.00

1921 Baltimore, Md. . . . $20.00

ENVELOPES

1914 Cincinnati, Ohio $30.00
(printed on both sides)

1917 Montgomery, Alabama . . $50.00
(very desirable back of envelope printing)

1903 Jacksonville, Fla. $20.00

c.1912 Anniston, Alabama $15.00

1907 Hattiesburg, Miss. $25.00

Early 1900 Waycross, Georgia,
Return Postcard $20.00

1904 Montgomery, Ala. . . $25.00

1919 Camden, Ark. $40.00
(Very unusual, showing both bottles.
Note misspelled "Coco-Cola")

1937 Holdrege, Nebraska $10.00
(unusual, non-standard hand and bottle design)

1927 Piqua, Ohio $5.00
(standard hand and bottle design)

1931 St. Louis, Mo. $5.00
(standard hand and bottle design)

1936 Buffalo, N.Y. $10.00
(standard hand and bottle, 50th Ann.)

ENVELOPES

1924 Asa Candler $30.00

1918 Lexington, Ky. . . . $15.00

c.1915 Indianapolis, Ind. . . . $25.00

1908 Danville, Va. $20.00

1920 The Coca-Cola Company $10.00

c.1920's Indianapolis, Ind. (back of envelope) . . $15.00

1919 The Coca-Cola Co., New York . . $10.00

1943 Fayetteville, N.C. . . . $5.00

c.1908 New York . . . $10.00

1950's Mexico $3.00

1940's (standard design) . . . $5.00

c.1930's Palmerton, Pa. $5.00
(standard hand and bottle design)

CHECKS

NOTE: Many of these checks are colorful and very collectible, but also very common.

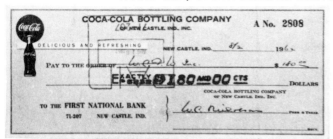

1962 New Castle, Ind. $2.00

1948 New Castle, Ind. $2.00

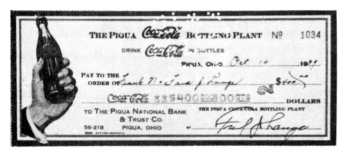

1939 Piqua, Oh. $3.00

1927 Newark, Oh. $4.00

1946 Dickson, Tenn. $3.00

1937 Dickson, Tenn. $3.00

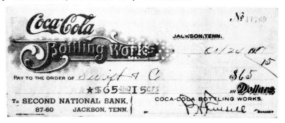

1927 Jackson, Tenn. $5.00

1917 Dickson, Tenn. $4.00

1919 Dickson, Tenn. $4.00

1958 Dickson, Tenn. $2.00

1923 Dickson, Tenn. $4.00

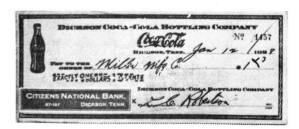

1928 Dickson, Tenn. $4.00

STOCK CERTIFICATES

1934 Coca-Cola Bottling Sales Co.   . . $75.00

1929 10 shares $75.00

1930's Blank Certificate $20.00

1958 10 Shares $20.00

1958 100 Shares $20.00

MISCELLANEOUS

1920's Glass advertising slides
(hand colored) . . . . . $65.00 Each

1920's "Radiator Plate" chrome 17" $225.00

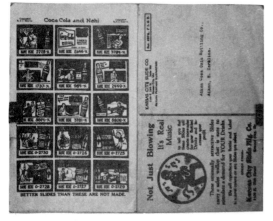

Early 1930's Folder and order form from
Kansas City Slide Co., showing Coca-Cola
and other advertising slides $65.00

1911
List of Bottler's Advertising Matter

The Coca-Cola Bottling Co.
233 CANDLER BUILDING
Atlanta, Ga.

1911 Spring Calendars (Ready Feb. 15th) Motor Girl . . . . .each .10
1911 Spring Hangers (Ready Feb. 15th) Motor Girl . . . . .each .08
1911 Postal Cards (Ready Feb. 15th) Motor Girl . . . . per M. 3.00
1911 Litho. Blotters (Ready Feb. 15th) Motor Girl (Env. Size) . . . . per M. 3.00
1911 Pocket Mirrors (Ready Feb. 15th) Motor Girl . . . . .each .02
1911 Watch Fobs (Ready Feb. 15th) Motor Girl . . . . .each .08
1911 Match Cases (Ready Feb. 15th) Motor Girl . . . . .each .05
Street Car Cards, 1910 Girl . . . . .each .05
Playing Cards, 1910 Girl, plain edge . . . . . . .pack .20
Playing Cards, 1910 Girl, gilt edge . . . . .pack .25
Window Transfer Signs, 1910 Girl . . . . . . .each .05
Caps, White Leatherette . . . . .each .08
Slate Books . . . . .each .03
Pencils (Packed six dozen to box) . . . . . . .dozen .30
Coin Purses . . . . .each .23
1911 Card Cases . . . . .each .20
Pocket Knives, Large Combination . . . . .each .90
Pocket Knives, 1911 Special . . . . .each .60
Pocket Knives, Small . . . . .each .30
Large Eight-Day Clocks . . . . .each 2.75
Desk Clocks, Special 1911 Bottle (Ready March 1, 1911) . . . . .each 1.25
Blotters, Large Size . . . . .per M. 1.50
Key Ring Openers . . . . .per M. 12.50
Coca-Cola Umbrellas . . . . .each 1.25
Bottle Pyramids (For Counter Display) Collapsible . . . . .each .20
Fibre Signs 18x120, with Bottle . . . . .each .13
Fibre Signs 15x48, with Bottle . . . . .each .04
Fibre Signs 18x48 (with Bottler's name) . . . .each .05
Fibre Signs 15x24 (Ice Cold Coca-Cola in Bottles) . . . . .each .02
Oil Cloth Signs 12x144, Bottlers . . . . .each .30
Oil Cloth Signs 18x48, with Bottle . . . . . .each .12
Metal Signs 12x36, with Bottle . . . . .each .15
Metal Signs 6x24 . . . . .each .05
Labels . . . . .case 10.00

1911 Price List of bottlers
advertising matter . . $50.00

NOTE: Pre-1920 bottlers price lists are very interesting and useful for dating and identifying pieces.

The 1911 price list shown above is particularly interesting because it identifys the so called "Duster Girl" as the "Motor Girl".

These early price lists are rare.

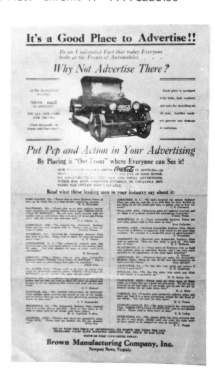

1920's Advertising and testimonial
sheet from Brown Mfg., regarding
"Radiator Plates" $50.00

1920's Profit Sharing poster
and coupons $35.00

1928 Icy-O Cooler sheet
showing different coolers . . $35.00

MISCELLANEOUS

c.1908
Coca-Cola
Bottling Co.,
Goldelle Ginger Ale label . . $35.00

c.1912 (Early motion picture)
"Verigraph" glasses, Rare $400.00

1920's "Tickletoes"
The Wonder Doll coupon . $50.00

1930's Cigar Bands(glass & bottle). $75.00 Each

March 13,1929 Sioux City Tribune (complete newspaper)
announcing death of Asa G. Candler $150.00

1930 Atlanta, Ga., Bottlers
Conference Program . $10.00

1934 Century of Progress Ticket
Free Coke offer on rev. . . $25.00

c.1929 Trolley Transfer . . . $2.00

"Coca-Cola Baby Doll" Cardboard Cutout
4"X 9½" $150.00

1941 San Antonio, Tx.
Bottlers Conference
Program $8.00

1925 Needle Case $40.00

Inside of Needle Case (folder) same on both 1924 & 1925

1924 Needle Case $40.00

MISCELLANEOUS

1964 Christmas Party Poem folder . . . $10.00

1964 Worlds Fair folder . . $4.00

1968 "Coca-Cola Day" ticket . . . $3.00

1940's Edgar Bergen (Canada) Free bottles offer $8.00

1950's "Birthday Card" Free Drink offer . . $10.00

Late 1920's "Thomas" Free bottle coupon $2.00

1940's "Safety Rules" Sheet (Canada) $2.00

1943 "America's Fighting Planes" set of 20 cards in envelope 2"X 3" $30.00

1950's "Coke Caps" envelope . . . $4.00

1941 Cavalier Coolers folder $10.00

1930's "Nature Study Cards"
Complete set in box $35.00
Individual packs with wrapper . . $5.00
Individual cards . . . . .75 Each

1940's "Birthday Card" Free Drink offer . . $10.00

c.1930 . . . $50.00

1961 . . . $25.00

1959 . . . $35.00

1955 . . . . $25.00

CONVENTION BADGES

-263-

MISCELLANEOUS

c.1915 "Accept No Imitations" Confederate Souvenir Bill $75.00

c.1920 "Accept No Imitations" Confederate Souvenir Bill $50.00

1931 "Accept No Imitations" Confederate Souvenir Bill $35.00
(United Confederate Veterans Reunion)

1932 FAMOUS DOCTORS SERIES
6 to the set

Heavy paper folders 12"X 17" open 8½"X 12" closed

1. Hippocrates 2. William Harvey 3. Louis Pasteur
4. Lord Lister 5. W.C. Rontgen 6. Walter Reed

Individuals . . $10.00   Complete Set of 6 . . . . . . $75.00

c.1910 Waycross Case Tag . . $15.00

c.1910 Panama City Case Tag . $15.00

c.1920 Bogalusa Case Tag . . . $5.00

c.1920's Owensboro Case Tag . $5.00

c.1920's Lexington Case Tag . $5.00

c.1920's Ronceverte Case Tag . $3.00

BOTTLE SHIPPING CASE ADDRESS TAGS

PLANT TOUR SOUVENIRS

1960's Case, 3½"X 6" . . $5.00

Both of these are
fan out paper tour
guides.

1950's Bottle, 6½" . . $5.00

NO-DRIP BOTTLE PROTECTORS

The "No-Drip Bottle Protector" or "Dry Server" is a paper sleeve that would fit over an iced bottle to keep your hand dry. These were used from the late 1920's up into the 1940's. Electric coolers eliminated the need for the "Bottle Bags" (as they are sometimes called). All pictured are 3 7/8"X 6 ¾", unless noted. An attempt has been made to put these in chronological order and to note the advertising slogan, for reference purposes. Of course any design might be used over several years, but believe these dates would be approximately correct. I have seen other designs not shown below. These may often be bought for 25c to $1.00 each, as they have a tendency to turn up in large quantities.　　　Courtesy: Thom Thompson, Versailles, Ky.

c.1929 . . . . $6.00
"Pause That Refreshes"
2 7/8"X 6"

c.1929 . . . . $5.00
"Dry Server"
2¾"X 6"

c.1930 . . . . $3.00
"In Bottles"

c.1931 . . . . $5.00
"Our Sandwiches
Delicious with Ice Cold"

c.1934 . . . . $4.00
"Good Things To Eat"
(A)

c.1934 . . . . $4.00
"Good Things To Eat"
(B)

c.1936 . . . . $5.00
"The Pause That
Refreshes"

c.1936 . . . . $5.00
"And Now. . The Pause
That Refreshes"

c.1938 . . . . $5.00
"A Great Drink With
Good Things To Eat"

c.1930's, 2 different dispensers for the "No-Drip Protectors", would fasten to the side of coolers. These are NOT marked "Coca-Cola". Values . . . . . $35.00 and $50.00

c.1938 . . . . $4.00
"So Refreshing
With Food"

c.1940 . . . . $4.00
"The Drink Everybody
Knows" (A)

c.1940 . . . . $4.00
"The Drink Everybody
Knows" (B)

c.1942 . . . . $4.00
"So Easy To Serve
At Home"

c.1942 . . . . $4.00
"When You Entertain"

c.1942 . . . . $4.00
"Thirst Asks Nothing
More"

c.1944 . . . . $3.00
"Makes A Light
Lunch Refreshing"

c.1944 . . . . $3.00
"Home Refreshment"

c.1946 . . . . $2.00
"Take A Minute
To Refresh" (A)

c.1946 . . . . $2.00
"Take A Minute
To Refresh" (B)

c.1946 . . . . $2.00
"A Great Drink
With Lunch"

c.1946 . . . . $3.00
"The Taste That
Always Charms"

c.1946 . . . . $3.00
"Take Off Refreshed"

c.1948 . . . . $5.00
"It's The Real Thing"

c.1948 . . . . $5.00
"Refreshment Right
Out Of The Bottle"

c.1948 . . . . $4.00
"Every Bottle Refreshes"

CHRISTMAS CARDS

1920's $15.00

1920's $15.00

Late 1920's $10.00

c.1935 . . . . . $5.00

Early 1940's $5.00

1935 . . . . $8.00

Early 1940's . . . $5.00

1936 . . . . . $5.00

COCA-COLA AND SPORTS

1920's Glass advertising slide (Lew McCarty)
Brooklyn Dodgers $125.00

1939 "100 Years of Baseball" . . $250.00
21"X 28" paper poster, metal strips top and
bottom, history of baseball, records, pictures
hall of fame players, shows 1939 schedule.
(printed both sides)

1940 Paper Poster $250.00
17"X 31", metal strips top and bottom,
recaps 1939 baseball season, pictures 1939
All Stars, with additional records and
historical data, shows 1940 schedule.
(printed both sides)

1910 Baseball Record Book . . $125.00

1933 St. Petersburg, Fla. (Photo)
Softball Team with
Buster Keaton in center . . $25.00

1920's Coca-Cola Baseball team photo
$35.00

1938 and 1940
Horse Racing Programs
with Coke Ads . . . $30.00 Each

1932 "Boston Garden News" Ad . . $45.00

1926 Coca-Cola Canada (Photo)
Local Hockey Team $30.00

1936-37 Basketball
Score Book . . . $25.00

1960 "Hall of Fame Records" showing both sides, American and National leagues $30.00

$75.00 $125.00

1932 "Olympic Record Indicator" showing both sides of two different examples.

1960's Boating Guide . . $5.00

1980 (Topps) set of 11 Champion Phillies $10.00

1907 Baseball Scorekeeper . . . $50.00

1949 "Baseball Rules" booklet $5.00

1930 Jersey City, N.J. Baseball Program . . $20.00

1970's Coca-Cola USA "Great Olympic Moments" coin set $15.00

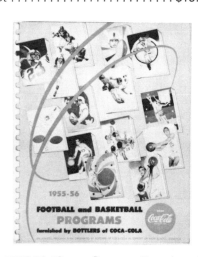

1955-56 "Sports Programs" catalog of samples and prices $25.00

1950's Sports Programs . . . . $5.00 Each

BASEBALL CARDS
1952 Coca-Cola Baseball card carton inserts.
Individual cards . . . $20.00 Each   Complete set of 10 . . . . $250.00

Coke is a Natural!

WES WESTRUM
GIANT CATCHER

SEE BACK OF CARD FOR
BIG-LEAGUE POINTERS ON HOW
TO BE A GOOD CATCHER

GIANTS AT HOME 1952

May 15, 16, 17 .... Chicago
May 18 (2), 19 .... Pittsburgh
May 20●, 21, 22 .... St. Louis
May 23●, 24, 25 .... Boston
May 26● .... Brooklyn
June 14, 15, 2●, 16 ... St. Louis
June 17●, 19 .... Pittsburgh
June 20●, 21, 22 (2) ... Chicago
June 23, 24●, 25 .... Cincinnati
July 4, 2 .... Brooklyn
July 5, 6, ●2 .... Philadelphia
July 22●, 24 .... St. Louis
July 25, 26, 27, 2 ..... Cincinnati
July 29●, 31 .... Chicago
Aug 1●, 2, 3 .... Pittsburgh
Aug 5●, 6, 7 .... Brooklyn
Aug 15●, 16, 17, 2● ... Boston
Sept 3●, 5 .... Philadelphia
Sept 6, 7 .... Brooklyn
Sept 9, 10, 11 .... Pittsburgh
Sept 12, 13 .... Cincinnati
Sept 14, 15 .... St. Louis
Sept 16, 17 .... Chicago
Sept 23, 24 .... Boston
Sept 26, 27, 28 .... Philadelphia
● NIGHT   (2) Two games

COLLECT ALL 10 BIG-LEAGUE
BASEBALL CARDS

Coke is a Natural!

BOBBY THOMSON
GIANT 3rd BASEMAN

SEE BACK OF CARD FOR
BIG-LEAGUE POINTERS ON HOW
TO BE A GOOD THIRD BASEMAN

GIANTS AT HOME 1952

May 15, 16, 17 .... Chicago
May 18 (2), 19 .... Pittsburgh
May 20●, 21, 22 .... St. Louis
May 23●, 24, 25 .... Boston
May 26● .... Brooklyn
June 14, 15, 2●, 16 ... St. Louis
June 17●, 19 .... Pittsburgh
June 20●, 21, 22, 2 ... Chicago
June 23, 24●, 25 .... Cincinnati
July 4, 2 .... Brooklyn
July 5, 6, 2 .... Philadelphia
July 22●, 24 .... St. Louis
July 25, 26, 27, 2 ..... Cincinnati
July 29●, 31 .... Chicago
Aug 1●, 2, 3 .... Pittsburgh
Aug 5●, 6, 7 .... Brooklyn
Aug 15●, 16, 17, 2 .... Boston
Sept 3●, 5 .... Philadelphia
Sept 6, 7 .... Brooklyn
Sept 9, 10, 11 .... Pittsburgh
Sept 12, 13 .... Cincinnati
Sept 14, 15 .... St. Louis
Sept 16, 17 .... Chicago
Sept 23, 24 .... Boston
Sept 26, 27, 28 .... Philadelphia
● NIGHT   (2) Two games

COLLECT ALL 10 BIG-LEAGUE
BASEBALL CARDS

Coke is a Natural!

GIL McDOUGALD
YANKEE 2nd BASEMAN

SEE BACK OF CARD FOR
BIG-LEAGUE POINTERS ON HOW
TO BE A GOOD SECOND BASEMAN

YANKEES AT HOME 1952

May 27 .... Washington
May 29, 30, 2● .... Philadelphia
May 31 .... Cleveland
June 1, 2 .... Cleveland
June 3●, 4, 5 .... Chicago
June 6, 7, 8, 2 .... St. Louis
June 10●, 11, 12 ...... Detroit
June 27●, 28 .... Philadelphia
June 29, 2 .... Washington
June 30 .... Boston
July 1●, 2 .... Boston
July 10●, 11, 12 ...... St. Louis
July 13, 2, 14 .... Detroit
July 15●, 16, 17 ...... Cleveland
July 18, 19, 20 .... Chicago
July 21● .... Brooklyn
Aug 8●, 9, 10 .... Boston
Aug 12●, 13, 14 ...... Washington
Aug 19●, 20, 21 ...... Chicago
Aug 22, 23 .... Cleveland
Aug 26●, 27 .... Detroit
Aug 28, 30, 31 .... Washington
Sept 1, 2 .... Boston
Sept 19●, 20, 21 ..... Philadelphia
● NIGHT   (2) Two games

COLLECT ALL 10 BIG-LEAGUE
BASEBALL CARDS

Coke is a Natural!

GIL HODGES
DODGER 1st BASEMAN

SEE BACK OF CARD FOR
BIG-LEAGUE POINTERS ON HOW
TO BE A GOOD FIRST BASEMAN

DODGERS AT HOME 1952

May 15●, 16, 17 .... Pittsburgh
May 18, 19● .... Chicago
May 20, 21●, 22 ...... Cincinnati
May 27●, 28 .... New York
May 29, 30, 2 .... Boston
June 14, 14●, 2, 15 .. Cincinnati
June 17●, 18, 19 ..... Chicago
June 20, 21●, 22 ..... Pittsburgh
June 23●, 24, 25 ..... St. Louis
June 27●, 28●, 29 ... Boston
June 30 .... Philadelphia
July 1, 2 .... Philadelphia
July 3 .... New York
July 22●, 23, 24 ..... Cincinnati
July 25●, 26, 27, 28● . St. Louis
July 29●, 30, 31 ..... Pittsburgh
Aug 1, 2, 3 .... Chicago
Aug 12●, 13, 14 ...... New York
Aug 15●, 16, 17 ...... Philadelphia
Aug 30●, 31 .... New York
Sept 9●, 10, 11 ...... Chicago
Sept 12●, 13 .... St. Louis
Sept 14, 15 .... Cincinnati
Sept 16, 17 .... Pittsburgh
Sept 23 .... Philadelphia
Sept 26, 27, 28 .... Boston
● NIGHT   (2) Two games

COLLECT ALL 10 BIG-LEAGUE
BASEBALL CARDS

Coke is a Natural!

HANK BAUER
YANKEE OUTFIELDER

SEE BACK OF CARD FOR
BIG-LEAGUE POINTERS ON HOW
TO BE A GOOD FIELDER

YANKEES AT HOME 1952

May 27 .... Washington
May 29, 30, 2 .... Philadelphia
May 31 .... Cleveland
June 1, 2 .... Cleveland
June 3●, 4, 5 .... Chicago
June 6, 7, 8, 2 .... St. Louis
June 10●, 11, 12 ...... Detroit
June 27●, 28 .... Philadelphia
June 29, 2 .... Washington
June 30 .... Boston
July 1●, 2 .... Boston
July 10●, 11, 12 ...... St. Louis
July 13, 2, 14 .... Detroit
July 15●, 16, 17 ...... Cleveland
July 18, 19, 20 .... Chicago
July 21● .... Brooklyn
Aug 8●, 9, 10 .... Boston
Aug 12●, 13, 14 ...... Washington
Aug 19●, 20, 21 ...... Chicago
Aug 22, 23 .... Cleveland
Aug 26●, 27 .... Detroit
Aug 28, 30, 31 .... Washington
Sept 1, 2 .... Boston
Sept 19●, 20, 21 ..... Philadelphia
● NIGHT   (2) Two games

COLLECT ALL 10 BIG-LEAGUE
BASEBALL CARDS

Coke is a Natural!

ED LOPAT
YANKEE PITCHER

SEE BACK OF CARD FOR
BIG-LEAGUE POINTERS ON HOW
TO BE A GOOD PITCHER

YANKEES AT HOME 1952

May 27 .... Washington
May 29, 30, 2 .... Philadelphia
May 31 .... Cleveland
June 1, 2 .... Cleveland
June 3●, 4, 5 .... Chicago
June 6, 7, 8, 2 .... St. Louis
June 10●, 11, 12 ...... Detroit
June 27●, 28 .... Philadelphia
June 29, 2 .... Washington
June 30 .... Boston
July 1●, 2 .... Boston
July 10●, 11, 12 ...... St. Louis
July 13, 2, 14 .... Detroit
July 15●, 16, 17 ...... Cleveland
July 18, 19, 20 .... Chicago
July 21● .... Brooklyn
Aug 8●, 9, 10 .... Boston
Aug 12●, 13, 14 ...... Washington
Aug 19●, 20, 21 ...... Chicago
Aug 22, 23 .... Cleveland
Aug 26●, 27 .... Detroit
Aug 28, 30, 31 .... Washington
Sept 1, 2 .... Boston
Sept 19●, 20, 21 ..... Philadelphia
● NIGHT   (2) Two games

COLLECT ALL 10 BIG-LEAGUE
BASEBALL CARDS

Coke is a Natural!

BOBBY THOMSON
GIANT 3rd BASEMAN

SEE BACK OF CARD FOR
BIG-LEAGUE POINTERS ON
HITTING

GIANTS AT HOME 1952

May 15, 16, 17 .... Chicago
May 18, 2, 19 .... Pittsburgh
May 20●, 21, 22 .... St. Louis
May 23●, 24, 25 .... Boston
May 26● .... Brooklyn
June 14, 15, 2, 16 .... Brooklyn
June 17●, 19 .... Pittsburgh
June 20●, 21, 22, 2 ... Chicago
June 23, 24●, 25 .... Cincinnati
July 4, 2 .... Brooklyn
July 5, 6, 2 .... Philadelphia
July 22●, 24 .... St. Louis
July 25, 26, 27, 2 ..... Cincinnati
July 29●, 31 .... Chicago
Aug 1●, 2, 3 .... Pittsburgh
Aug 5●, 6, 7 .... Brooklyn
Aug 15●, 16, 17, 2 .... Boston
Sept 3●, 5 .... Philadelphia
Sept 6, 7 .... Brooklyn
Sept 9, 10, 11 .... Pittsburgh
Sept 12, 13 .... Cincinnati
Sept 14, 15 .... St. Louis
Sept 16, 17 .... Chicago
Sept 23, 24 .... Boston
Sept 26, 27, 28 .... Philadelphia
● NIGHT   (2) Two games

COLLECT ALL 10 BIG-LEAGUE
BASEBALL CARDS

Coke is a Natural!

CARL FURILLO
DODGER OUTFIELDER

SEE BACK OF CARD FOR
BIG-LEAGUE POINTERS ON HOW
TO BE A GOOD FIELDER

DODGERS AT HOME 1952

May 15●, 16, 17 .... Pittsburgh
May 18, 19● .... Chicago
May 20, 21●, 22 ...... Cincinnati
May 27●, 28 .... New York
May 29, 30, 2 .... Boston
June 14, 14●, 2, 15 .. Cincinnati
June 17●, 18, 19 ..... Chicago
June 20, 21●, 22 ..... Pittsburgh
June 23●, 24, 25 ..... St. Louis
June 27●, 28●, 29 ... Boston
June 30 .... Philadelphia
July 1, 2 .... Philadelphia
July 3 .... New York
July 22●, 23, 24 ..... Cincinnati
July 25●, 26, 27, 28● . St. Louis
July 29●, 30, 31 ..... Pittsburgh
Aug 1, 2, 3 .... Chicago
Aug 12●, 13, 14 ...... New York
Aug 15●, 16, 17 ...... Philadelphia
Aug 30●, 31 .... New York
Sept 9●, 10, 11 ...... Chicago
Sept 12●, 13 .... St. Louis
Sept 14, 15 .... Cincinnati
Sept 16, 17 .... Pittsburgh
Sept 23 .... Philadelphia
Sept 26, 27, 28 .... Boston
● NIGHT   (2) Two games

COLLECT ALL 10 BIG-LEAGUE
BASEBALL CARDS

Coke is a Natural!

DON MUELLER
GIANT OUTFIELDER

SEE BACK OF CARD FOR
BIG-LEAGUE POINTERS ON HOW
TO BE A GOOD FIELDER

GIANTS AT HOME 1952

May 15, 16, 17 .... Chicago
May 18, 2, 19 .... Pittsburgh
May 20●, 21, 22 .... St. Louis
May 23●, 24, 25 .... Boston
May 26● .... Brooklyn
June 14, 15, 2, 16 .... St. Louis
June 17●, 19 .... Pittsburgh
June 20●, 21, 22, 2 ... Chicago
June 23, 24●, 25 .... Cincinnati
July 4, 2 .... Brooklyn
July 5, 6, 2 .... Philadelphia
July 22●, 24 .... St. Louis
July 25, 26, 27, 2 ..... Cincinnati
July 29●, 31 .... Chicago
Aug 1●, 2, 3 .... Pittsburgh
Aug 5●, 6, 7 .... Brooklyn
Aug 15●, 16, 17, 2 .... Boston
Sept 3●, 5 .... Philadelphia
Sept 6, 7 .... Brooklyn
Sept 9, 10, 11 .... Pittsburgh
Sept 12, 13 .... Cincinnati
Sept 14, 15 .... St. Louis
Sept 16, 17 .... Chicago
Sept 23, 24 .... Boston
Sept 26, 27, 28 .... Philadelphia
● NIGHT   (2) Two games

COLLECT ALL 10 BIG-LEAGUE
BASEBALL CARDS

Coke is a Natural!

PEEWEE REESE
DODGER SHORTSTOP

SEE BACK OF CARD FOR
BIG-LEAGUE POINTERS ON HOW
TO BE A GOOD SHORTSTOP

DODGERS AT HOME 1952

May 15●, 16, 17 .... Pittsburgh
May 18, 19● .... Chicago
May 20, 21●, 22 ...... Cincinnati
May 27●, 28 .... New York
May 29, 30, (2) .... Boston
June 14, 14●, 2, 15 .. Cincinnati
June 17●, 18, 19 ..... Chicago
June 20, 21●, 22 ..... Pittsburgh
June 23●, 24, 25 ..... St. Louis
June 27●, 28●, 29 ... Boston
June 30 .... Philadelphia
July 1, 2 .... Philadelphia
July 3 .... New York
July 22●, 23, 24 ..... Cincinnati
July 25●, 26, 27, 28● . St. Louis
July 29●, 30, 31 ..... Pittsburgh
Aug 1, 2, 3 .... Chicago
Aug 12●, 13, 14 ...... New York
Aug 15●, 16, 17 ...... Philadelphia
Aug 30●, 31 .... New York
Sept 9●, 10, 11 ...... Chicago
Sept 12●, 13 .... St. Louis
Sept 14, 15 .... Cincinnati
Sept 16, 17 .... Pittsburgh
Sept 23 .... Philadelphia
Sept 26, 27, 28 .... Boston
● NIGHT   (2) Two games

COLLECT ALL 10 BIG-LEAGUE
BASEBALL CARDS

BASEBALL SCORE CARDS

1916 Chicago & St. Louis . . $150.00

1957 Dodgers $15.00

1946 Athletics $25.00

1944 Athletics $25.00

1942 St. Louis Cards . . $25.00

1942 St. Louis Browns . . $25.00

1947 Athletics $20.00

NOTE: These Score Cards are very collectible and interesting. Keep in mind that some may be worth more to a baseball collector than to a coke collector. A World Series card would be a good example.

1964 Red Sox $10.00

1949 Cardinals $10.00

1942 Athletics $20.00

BASEBALL SCORE CARDS

1961 Red Sox $12.00

1963 Yankees . . $20.00

1960 Orioles $10.00

1963 Mets $10.00

NOTE: Baseball Score Cards can make a great collection, they're basically inexpensive, very interesting and easy to find. Any good baseball card show, should have many to choose from.

1951 Athletics $15.00

1952 Pittsburg Pirates $12.00

1952 Athletics $12.00

1966 Red Sox $10.00

1950 Chicago Cubs $10.00

ADVERTISING MANUALS AND PRICE LISTS

1927 Bottlers Price List $125.00

1950's Advertising Price List . . $100.00
(Price based on near complete book)

1934 Bottler Price List $175.00

NOTE:
Prices on these books and manuals vary depending on contents.

1920's Bottlers Price List . . . $150.00

1940's Advertising Manual $175.00

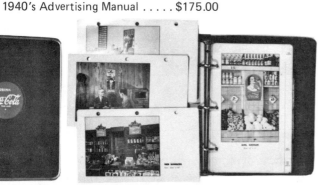

1938 Advertising Manual $125.00
(Price based on near complete book)

1960's Advertising Manual $125.00
(Price based on near complete book)

ADVERTISING MANUALS, INSTRUCTION FOLDERS, ETC.

1930's folder showing display
pieces available $20.00

1936 window display
instruction folder . . . $20.00

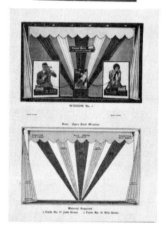

1931 Standardized Delivery
Equipment booklet . . $100.00

1950 Product Book (showing items
available that year) $25.00

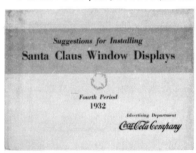

1932 and 1933 Window Display instruction folders . . . $25.00 Each

1930 Telephone Window Display
instruction booklet $35.00

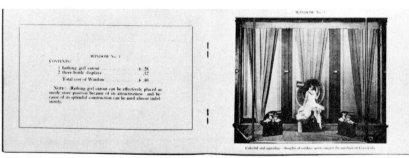

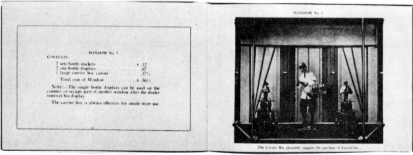

1926 Booklet showing window displays, description,
prices and layouts $60.00

c.1909 "Window Displays for Druggists"
book showing store window displays
(not a Coca-Cola publication) . . . $50.00

WINDOW DISPLAY INSTRUCTION BOOKLETS

1928 Summer Display . . $45.00

1929 Orchid Display . . $45.00

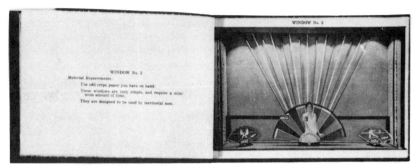

1926 Fan Display $50.00

1926 Window Displays . . . $60.00

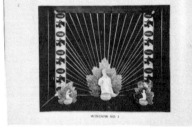

1927 Fall Window Displays $50.00

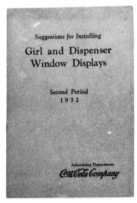

1932 Girl and Dispenser . . $40.00

1928 Bench Display . . $50.00

1932 Olympic Display . . $45.00

Cigar Band page only . . $25.00

Feb. 1933
Fortune Magazine
with cigar band
insert page, featuring a
Coca-Cola Cigar Band $40.00

1927 Newspaper Advertising
Tear Sheet $25.00

1928 "A Letter" booklet
and insert pieces concerning
the new 6 pack box $100.00

1950 Newspaper
Advertising book . . $25.00

1950's Westinghouse
Coolers Catalog . . $10.00

1950's Coolers
Sales Tips . . $10.00

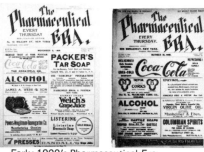

Early 1900's Pharmaceutical Era
Magazine with Coke Ads . . $25.00 Each

1928 Outdoor Sign Painting
Specification Catalog . . $20.00

1927 . . . $25.00

1926 . . . $25.00

1930 . . . $10.00

1928 . . . $12.00

RAND McNALLY ROAD MAPS

BOOKS, CATALOGS, ADVERTISING MANUALS

1936 "What Happend in Atlanta" bottlers conference material $25.00

1912-1915 "Dime Novels" with color Coca-Cola ads on back covers. . . $5.00 - $20.00 Each

(Price depends on ad and condition of book)

NOTE: Many of these Dime Novels have copyright dates much earlier than the actual printing of the book. This date refers to the copyright of the story, not the book or ad.

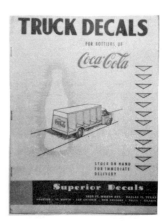

1960's "Truck Decals" brochure $10.00

1940's U.S. Army note pad . . . $5.00

Late 60's Early 70's Golden Legacy Magazines . . $3.00 Each

1958-1961 Pause for Living bound volume $10.00

1940's "Radio Material" booklet . . $8.00

1930's "These Changing Times" Soda Fountain Book . $12.00

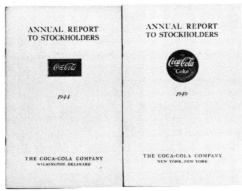

1940's Annual Report to stockholders . . $10.00 Each

1934 Western Bottlers Conference program $15.00

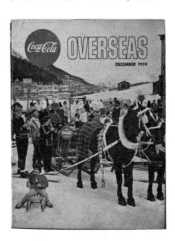

1959 Coca-Cola "Overseas" . . $5.00

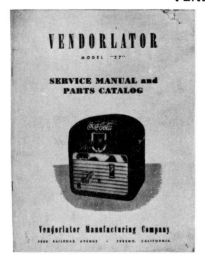

Vendorlator Model 27 . . . $25.00

Vendo Parts and Service Manual
$20.00

1939 - 1940
Vendo
Parts and Service
Manuals
$20.00 Each

1936 - 1941
Cavalier
Parts Catalog
$10.00 - $15.00 Each

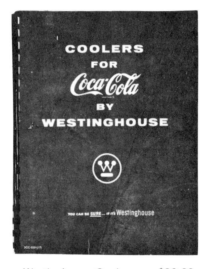

Westinghouse Coolers . . . $20.00

Vendo V-83 . . . $15.00

NOTE: These manuals are especially interesting and sought after by collectors who specialize in vending machines, and often pay premium prices for particular manuals.

Mills Model 45 . . . $20.00

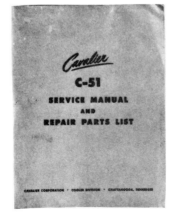

Cavalier C-51 . . . $10.00

1940 Mills $20.00

Vendo V39 . . . . $15.00

THE COCA-COLA BOTTLER AND RED BARREL MAGAZINE

Both "The Coca-Cola Bottler" and "Red Barrel" are company publications, directed to bottlers, company employees, and executives. All of these publications are very difficult to price, because the contents vary so much. If the magazine shows alot of interesting advertising, it could be worth more than my estimate.

1934 . . . $125.00
(Complete year, bound)

March, 1945. $7.00

May, 1933 . . $20.00

Aug., 1943 . . . $7.00

May, 1934, w/envelope . . $25.00

Dec., 1940 . . . $7.00

Dec., 1941 . . . $7.00

Sept., 1941 . . . $7.00

Feb., 1943 . . . $7.00

Dec., 1942 . . . $7.00

1949 . . . . . . $10.00

1909 (reprint) $10.00
This was an insert in
the Coca-Cola Bottler
magazine (1959)
shown below.

Oct., 1938 . . $15.00

Jan., 1928 . . $20.00

NOTE: Both "The Coca-Cola Bottler"
and "Red Barrel" have a wealth of
information for the collector. Much
of the information that we have, as
far as dating and identifying advertising and production material has
come from these publications.

1959 50th Anniversary
Issue $25.00

1949 40th Anniversary
Issue $35.00

BOOKS AND SCORE PADS

1951
Easy Hospitality
$5.00

1944 Boy Scouts Handbook $10.00

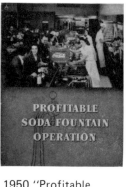

1950 "Profitable
Soda Fountain
Operation . . $4.00

1960's Touch Football
Rules Book . . . $5.00

1950's Comic Book $5.00

1950's Old Chips and
Charlie Comic . . . $5.00

1940's Our American
Neighbors . . . $5.00

1930's Visual Instruction
in Nature Study . . $8.00

1925 Websters
"Little Gem"
Dictionary
$30.00

1946 Group Life
Insurance Plan
booklet . . . $6.00

Score Pad
(Canada)
$3.00

c.1920's
Charm of
Purity . . $15.00

1915 "Coca-Cola
The Universal Beverage"
$200.00

1940's
World Atlas
$25.00

1929 "The Story of
Achievement in
Aviation" $50.00

BOOKS, NOTE AND SCORE PADS

1916 "THE ROMANCE
OF COCA-COLA . . $45.00

1928 "ALPHABET BOOK
OF COCA-COLA" $35.00

c.1912 "THE TRUTH ABOUT COCA-COLA"
16 PAGE BOOKLET $25.00

1923 "FACTS"
BOOK $35.00

1940's "KNOW YOUR
WAR PLANES" $30.00

1939 "MY DAILY REMINDER"
BOOKLET . . . $10.00

1932 "WHEN YOU ENTERTAIN"
By IDA BAILEY ALLEN . . . $8.00

1940's FLOWER ARRANGING BOOKS VOLUMES 1,2,3
By LAURA LEE BURROUGH . . . . $5.00 Each

1957 BOOK LISTING BOTTLERS
COMMEMORATING THEIR
50th ANNIVERSARY $20.00

1950's SPORTS
MANUAL
$5.00

1943-44 Notebook
$5.00

1940's SCORE PADS . . . . . $6.00 Each

1950's BRIDGE DIGEST
BOOKLET $8.00

1940 School Notebook (embossed cover) $40.00

1931 Note pad . . $25.00
(Norman Rockwell Art)

1937-1939 . . . $8.00

1936 50th Ann.$12.00

Late 1950's . . $3.00

1932-1935 . . $10.00

c.1920's Note Pad Holder
(for candle stick phone) . . . $50.00
(This piece always looks nice when displayed on a phone)

c.1940-1945 . . $5.00

1949-1950's . . $3.00

Early 1960's $4.00
(Atlanta Bottling Co.)

Late 1960's . . . $3.00

Late 1960's . . . $3.00

c.1960 . . . $3.00

Mid 1970's . . $2.00

1950's (Scarce) . . $25.00
Bottlers 50th Anniversary

Early 1970's . . $2.00

Late 1970's . . . $2.00

BOOK COVERS

1930-31 . . . . $5.00

1931 Rockwell Art $10.00

1950's $5.00

1939-40 . . . . $5.00

c.1937 . . . . $5.00

1950's $5.00

1960's $4.00

1950's $8.00

1960's Canada $4.00

1960's Canada $4.00

EDUCATIONAL MATERIAL

1940's "Map of North America" 30"X 36" . . . $35.00

1946 "Our America" Posters . . $20.00 Each

1946 "Our America" Booklets . . . . . $6.00 Each
Complete with unused stamps . . . . . $10.00 Each

DECALS AND STICKERS

1950's 10"X 10" Decal . . $25.00

1930's Menu Label
$10.00

1950's - 1960's 8"X 11" . . . . . . $10.00 Each

1970's Sticker . $1.00

1950's Decal $15.00

Early 1960's
Door Decal . . $10.00

PLEASE PAY CASHIER

1950's Decal . . . $5.00

1970's Bumper Sticker $2.00

Early 1970's Tab
Foil $5.00

1950's Coke "King Size"
Sticker $5.00

1950's Decal $5.00

1970's Foil $5.00

1960's Foil $8.00

APRONS, CAPS AND NECKTIES

1953 . . . $20.00

1950's-60's . . . $15.00

Early 50's . . $25.00

1970's . . . $10.00

1970's . . . $8.00

c.1920's Cloth Soda Jerk Cap . . $10.00

1940's Cloth Soda Jerk Cap . . $7.00

1950's Cardboard
Visor Cap $8.00

1950's Sprite Boy Paper Hat . . $10.00

1959
Beanie . . $20.00

1950 Baseball Cap
$7.00

1960's Cardboard
Visor Cap . . . $5.00

1940's Beanie . . $10.00

1930's Baseball Cap . . $30.00

1930's Beanie . . $20.00

1960's - 70's String Tie
$6.00

1970's . . . $8.00

1960's Western type Bow Tie
$10.00

1950's . . $60.00

1940's . $60.00

1960's . . . $30.00

CLOTHING

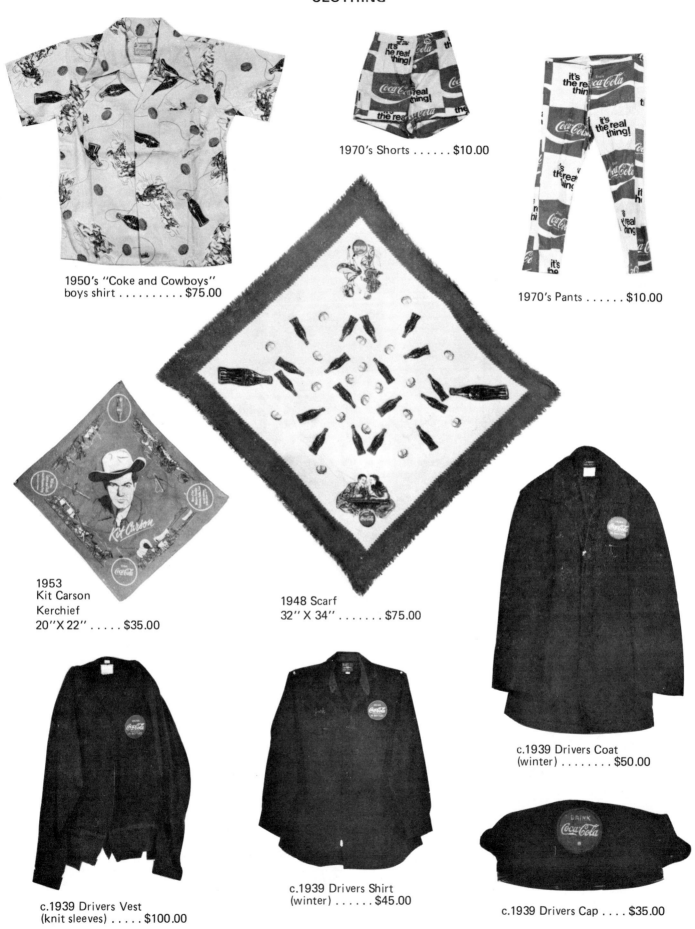

1970's Shorts $10.00

1970's Pants $10.00

1950's "Coke and Cowboys"
boys shirt $75.00

1953
Kit Carson
Kerchief
20" X 22" $35.00

1948 Scarf
32" X 34" $75.00

c.1939 Drivers Coat
(winter) $50.00

c.1939 Drivers Vest
(knit sleeves) $100.00

c.1939 Drivers Shirt
(winter) $45.00

c.1939 Drivers Cap $35.00

UNIFORM PATCHES

1950's . . . $6.00

1950's . . . $5.00

1960's . . . $4.00

1960's . . . $5.00

1920's . . . $35.00 Each

NOTE: Early uniforms, patches, and drivers caps are very collectable, and often difficult to find.

1950's Drivers Shirt $35.00

1960's . . $6.00

1960's . . . $4.00

1950's . . . $7.00

1960's . . . $4.00

1960's . . . $5.00

1960's . . . $5.00

1960's . . . $3.00

1976 . . $2.00

1950's - 1960's Large Back Patches . . . . $10.00 Each

1970 . . . $4.00

MAGAZINE ADS
The following ads are color Massengale.
(The Massengale Company was an advertising agency which produced many ads for The Coca-Cola Company.)

1906 . . $45.00

1907 . . $50.00

1907 . . $50.00

1906 . . $35.00

1906 . . $50.00

1906 . . $60.00

1907 . . $50.00

1906 . . $50.00

1906 . . $50.00

1906 . . $50.00

1907 . . $50.00

1907 . . $50.00

1905 . . $125.00

1905 . . $60.00

1905 . . $65.00

1905 . . . $35.00

1905 . . . $8.00

1904 . . . $15.00

1905 . . . $8.00

1906 . . . $8.00

1905 . . . $8.00

1906 . . . $30.00

1905 . . . $10.00

1905 . . . $8.00

1906 . . . $10.00

1906 . . . $10.00   1906 . . . $10.00

1906 . . . $30.00

MAGAZINE ADS
The following are black & white Massengale ads.

1907 . . . $30.00

1907 . . . $25.00

1907 . . . $15.00

1907 . . . $25.00

1907 . . . $15.00

1907 . . . $15.00

1907 . . . $25.00

1907 . . . $20.00

1907 . . . $15.00

1907 . . . $10.00

1907 . . . $15.00

1907 . . . $15.00

1907 . . . $40.00

MAGAZINE ADS

The following ads are color, front and back covers, from The Household and The People's Popular Monthly.

JUNE 1910 . . . $125.00

AUGUST 1911 . . . $100.00

AUGUST 1912 . . . $100.00

JULY 1913 . . . $100.00

AUGUST 1913 . . . $100.00

JUNE 1914 . . . $100.00

JULY 1914 . . . $100.00

MAY 1915 . . . $100.00

JULY 1916 . . . $100.00

JULY 1917 . . . $100.00

MAGAZINE ADS
The following ads are 2 color or full color.

1907 . . . $20.00

1912 . . . $6.00

1920 . . . $10.00

1912 . . . $8.00

1914 . . . $10.00

1915 . . . $10.00

1915 . . . $10.00

1917 . . . $6.00

1917 . . . $8.00

1915 . . . $10.00

1916 . . . $12.00

1916 . . . $10.00

1917 . . . $8.00

1917 . . . $8.00

1915 . . . $10.00

1915 . . . $10.00

MAGAZINE ADS

1909 2 color $8.00

Bulletin of Pharmacy
May 1913 B&W $25.00

1912 2 color $6.00

Bulletin of Pharmacy
June 1913 B&W $15.00

Bulletin of Pharmacy
June 1909 B&W $25.00

1907 B&W $10.00

1909 2 color $8.00

1909 Full color . . . $10.00

When the Sun
is Red Hot

1908 2 color $10.00

MAGAZINE ADS
The following ads are 2 color or full color.

1912 . . . $20.00

1916 . . . $20.00

1909 . . . $20.00

1908 . . . $18.00

1914 . . . $20.00

1912 . . . $10.00

1908 . . . $20.00

1908 . . . $20.00

1914 . . . $8.00

1914 . . . $6.00

1913 . . . $6.00

1914 . . . $8.00

1908 . . . $10.00

1914 . . . $6.00

1913 . . . $6.00

1909 . . . $20.00

MAGAZINE ADS
The following are 2 color, split column ads from Mother's Magazine.

1913 . . . $8.00

May 1915 . . . $10.00

May 1914 . . . $10.00

1913 . . . $10.00

June 1915 . . . $10.00

June 1913 . . . $10.00

June 1914 . . . $10.00

July 1915 . . . $10.00

May 1916 . . . $10.00

MAGAZINE ADS

The following are 2 color and black & white baseball player ads from American Boy Magazine.

August 1914 (2 color) . . . $35.00

1916 (2 color) . . . $20.00

July 1914 . . $15.00

June 1914
$15.00

May 1914 . . $15.00   Sept. 1914 . . $15.00

Sept. 1916 . $15.00   June 1916 . $15.00

May 1916 . $15.00   July 1916 . $15.00

1913 Full color $10.00

The People's Popular Monthly
front & back cover ad
June 1915 . . . . $100.00

1906 Scientific American
B&W $20.00

1920's Full color . . . $15.00

1914 2½" X 3½" Newspaper Ad . . $20.00

1907 B&W . . . $10.00

1906 B&W . . . $20.00

1907 2 color $15.00

International Trucks
Full color $20.00

1908 B&W $20.00

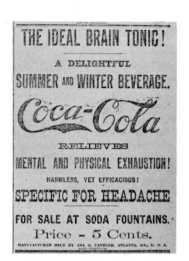

1891 4½'' x 6'' $200.00
pre-1900 ads are Rare

1907 .... $25.00

1907 .... $25.00

1906 .... $25.00

1906 .... $15.00

1915 11'' x 11'' $25.00

1910 .... $12.00

1910 7'' x 9'' $50.00

1903 2'' x 4'' $30.00

1906 .... $25.00

1904 .... $25.00

NEWSPAPER ADS
The following are B/W newspaper ads.

1906 . . . . $15.00

1906 . . . . $15.00

1906 . . . . $15.00

1907 10"x 15" $25.00

1907 10"x 15" $25.00

1915 9"x 13" . . . Rare . . $75.00
"Reunion of Confederate Soldiers"

1906 . . . . . $15.00

1911 . . . . . $15.00

1915 . . . . . . $15.00

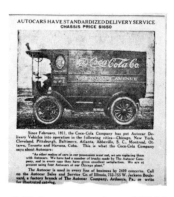

1915 Autocar trucks . . $10.00

NEWSPAPER ADS

The following B/W Baseball player ads are approx. 5"x 7". Take note that generally newspaper ads, because of brittleness and quality of printing are not worth as much as magazine ads.

1911 Hugh Jennings
Tigers $10.00

1911 Hans Wagner
Pitt. Pirates $10.00

1910 George Mullin
Detroit $10.00

1911 Fred Merkle . . $10.00

1910 George Gibson
Pitt. Nationals . . $10.00

1910 Jack O'Connor, Mgr.
St. Louis Americans . . $10.00

1910 Frank Chance
Cubs $10.00

1911 Del Howard
Louisville . . . $10.00

1910 Konetchy
St. Louis Cards . . . $10.00

1914 John Daubert
Brooklyn . . . $10.00

1914 John J. Evers
Boston Braves . . . $10.00

1906 Lajoie
Cleveland $10.00

NEWSPAPER ADS

The following B/W Baseball Player ads are approx. 5"x 7". Take note that generally newspaper ads, because of brittleness and quality of printing are not worth as much as magazine ads.

1913 Callahan
White Sox $10.00

1916 Fred Luderus
Phila. A's $10.00

1913 Slim Sallee
Cards $10.00

1915 Rabbit Maranville
Boston Braves $10.00

1916
Grover Cleveland Alexander
Phila. Nationals $10.00

1916 Joe Tinker
Cubs $10.00

1916 Larry Doyle
Cubs $10.00

1909 Connie Mack
Phila. A's $10.00

1916 Heine Zimmerman
Cubs $10.00

1915 Fireball Johnson
Wash. Nationals . . . $10.00

1916 Fielder Jones
Browns $10.00

1916 Carl Weilman
St. Louis Browns . . . $10.00

NEWSPAPER ADS

The following B/W Baseball player ads are approx. 5"x 7". Take note that generally newspaper ads, because of brittleness and quality of printing are not worth as much as magazine ads.

1910 Johnny Evers
Cubs $10.00

1912 Konetchy
St. Louis Cards . . $10.00

1912 Brainy Collins
Phila. A's $10.00

1909 Harry Davis
Phila. A's $10.00

1910 Skeets Dunleavy
Louisville . . . $25.00

1911 Dell Howard
Louisville 9"x 11" . . $25.00

1915 Cozy Dolan
St. Louis Browns . . $15.00

1906 "Athletes"
Coupon Ad . . . $15.00

1914 Walter Johnson
Wash. Senators . . . $12.00

1914 Collins
Phila. A's . . . $12.00

NEWSPAPER ADS

The following are full page (16"x 22") full color newspaper ads. Color newspaper ads are somewhat rare.

1931 . . . . $25.00

1933 Joan Crawford . . . $25.00

1931 . . . . $15.00

1936 . . . . $25.00

1936 . . . . $25.00

1931 . . . . $15.00

1935 . . . . $25.00

1932 . . . . $15.00

1931 . . . . $15.00

FANTASY AND REPRODUCTIONS

Many new, fantasy and reproduction items have fooled not only the novice but long time collector as well. It would be very difficult to show them all, however I've picked out some pieces that I've been asked about so often over the past few years. These items are NOT old. Keep in mind that this is only a very small sampling of the many hundreds of repro and fantasy items.

1970's Betty 28"X40" Pub Mirror
I've seen many different sizes and styles
of these mirrors and way over priced at $10.00 to $50.00

1970's Glass Oval Sign
I've seen 2 versions of this sign
$10.00 - $15.00

Betty Glass
Push Plate
NEW . . . $5.00

1970's Push Plate
I consider this piece
worthless, under $5.00

26"X34" Reproduction 1922 Festoon
(All one piece) Framed . . . $35.00

Belt Buckle
"Anson Mills"
Pat. Feb. 1, 1881
New $5.00

Straight Razor Etched Blade
$5.00

Pocket Watches
(Watch could be old
but dials are new)
Less than $10.00 Each

The Famous
"Nude Nun"
Belt Buckle
$5.00

Late 1970's 12"X 18" Pub Mirror
glass with wood frame $15.00

BELT BUCKLES
I've seen many styles and shapes of these belt buckles.
I've yet to see one that I would consider old . . . . $5.00 Each

FANTASY AND REPRODUCTIONS

1970's Glass Paperweight (Fantasy) $5.00
(This piece has been shown in other price guides as 1916 it is NOT old)

NOTE: I personally find all Fantasy items very objectionable. Many collectors have paid alot of money for these items, that are basically worthless. The prices you see on these items, are token prices, which in most cases I hesitate to give any value at all.

1980's (1923 Girl) Tray (Fantasy) . . . $5.00

1980's Made in Tiawan (Fantasy) Trays . . . . $1.00 Each

1970's "Pub Mirror" (Fantasy) $10.00

1980's "The Romance of Coca-Cola" (Fantasy) Trays . . . $5.00

FANTASY AND REPRODUCTIONS

Reproduction Signs (date unkown) overall size including matting 20"X 26" size of print only approx. 13¾"X 19½" These signs were framed and used in lobbies of bottling plants. Each sign has a small gold label under print identifying the model. These reproduction signs are one of the very few repro. items that I do approve of, they are very well done and very collectible. (produced by The Coca-Cola Co.)

Individual signs . . . . . $75.00 Each
Complete set of 4 . . . . $400.00

1970's Placemats, plastic coated . . . . $2.00 Each

(Set consists of 5 placemats, only 4 shown. "Motor Girl" missing.)

NOTE: Be very careful of these placemats. I have seen them cut down and framed and have fooled the unsuspecting.

Mid to Late 1970's Wire back ice cream chairs embossed metal seat (made in Mexico) . . . . $50.00 Each

NOTE: Many people think these chairs are old. I'm sorry to say they are NOT. I remember them coming into the market around the mid 1970's offered in set of 2 and sold for $50.00 per set.

1980's Tin Embossed sign 10¼"X 16½" . . $5.00

FANTASY AND REPRODUCTION

Recent Pocket Watch, (new face on old watch). This is a Fantasy item that's worth nothing as a Coca-Cola item, but rather what the watch is worth. . . $10.00 - $25.00

1980's Playing Cards (double deck) in tin and cardboard box. I've seen a few different versions of these cards. This is a Fantasy item at it's worst . . . . Worthless

Recent "Sprite Boy" Sewing Kit . . . $1.00

Reproduction Clock Face, on old clock. I've seen this face on many different types of clocks. Worth only what the clock is worth as a clock, Not as a Coke item.

Fantasy Glass Door Knobs (outline type logo) . . . Worthless

1970's - 80's Glass Dish (clear glass with white lettering). . . . . Worthless

"Owl" Coin in box, stamped in gold "1915 Convention" Not Old . . . $20.00

NOTE: You will notice I have listed some of these items as "Worthless". I do this because they are in such poor taste, designed to Rip-Off the collector, that I cannot in good conscience put a value on it.

Glass Paperweight $3.00

FANTASY AND REPRODUCTIONS

1914 CALENDAR TOP

ORIGINAL

REPRODUCTION

REPRODUCTION

ORIGINAL:

1. Size: 13''X 27''
2. Printed on a textured paper (because of the texture many people have mistakenly confused it with canvas).
3. Printed at bottom:
   at left — "Copyright the Coca-Cola Co."
   in center — "BETTY"
4. Value: $200.00 (top only)

REPRODUCTION:

1. Size: 11¼''X 23¾''
2. Printed on a smooth finish ivory heavy paper.
3. No printing at bottom.
4. Printed stain (obviously on original that this was photographed from) that covers the bottom right hand corner. (see photo right)
5. Printed crease across bottom.
6. Value: $2.00

NOTE: Often times when reproducing something the reproduction is reduced in size, (as is the 1914 calendar top by 87%) to sharpen up the quality. In this case as in most cases it didn't work. The quality is poor, however it's very difficult to tell that unless you've seen the original.
I know of many cases of this reproduction selling for hundreds of dollars. When it first appeared in the market place in the mid 1970's they sold for $2.00 each. I have given this piece a value of $2.00 very hesitantly, I do consider this piece worthless.

c.1970's 9 1/8''X 13¾'' Fantasy (heavy paper) sign . . . Worthless

Copy in lower left: "Copyright 1911 Coca-Cola Atlanta, Ga."
Copy in lower right: "Printed in U.S.A."

NOTE: This piece came on the market at the same time the repro "BETTY" calendar top. I suspect done by the same person. They originally sold for $2.00. I consider this piece worthless.

1980's Reproduction (masonite) 20''X 28'' sign . . $20.00

NOTE: Be careful!! this is an exact reproduction of the original masonite sign. Repro has a smooth back. Original has rough back.

FANTASY AND REPRODUCTIONS

Bottle shaped (cast) paperweight
Inside stamped 1938
Not Old $5.00

Original and old National Cash Register
with (Fantasy) Coca-Cola top & face plates.
Made in 2 sizes for large & small registers.
These plates add nothing to the value of an
original register.

Letter Opener (stamped metal)
Fantasy $2.00

Recent (Fantasy) street sign . . $5.00

Free Drink (stamped metal) Tokens
Fantasy some have bottle stamped
on reverse.
Not Old . . . . Worthless

NOTE: Silverware, carving sets,
knives, button hooks, hair brush-
es, hair receivers, etc. I've seen
everything imaginable. This stuff
is old but the stamping "Drink
Coca-Cola" has been added recently. . . . very little value.

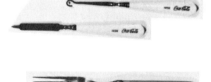

2 more examples of belt buckles
Fantasy . . . . $5.00 Each

Vendors Badge (stamped metal)
Not Old $3.00

FANTASY AND REPRODUCTION POCKET KNIVES

1970's - 80's Pocket Knives (Fantasy)
$1.00 to $2.00 Each
Pictured are just a few of the literally
hundreds of these similar knives on
the market.

c.1970's Bottle Shaped Pocket Knife, both brass and nickle handles. "Remington, U.M.C."
on blade. No original of this exist. Fantasy $8.00

c.1980's Round 2 blade knife. Mother
of pearl looking face (plastic) stamped
"U.S.A." on blade. Fantasy . . . $2.00

c.1980's Stamped metal. (similar to
knife at left) Fantasy $2.00

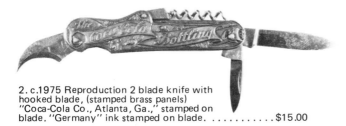

c.1980's Metal Bottle Shaped Knife.
Fantasy $2.00

c.1980's Metal "Boot" Pocket Knife.
Fantasy $2.00

The following 5 knives (4 pictured) are all recent reproductions of the 1905-1915 corkscrew pocket knives.
The dates are approximate first appearance in market place.

1. c.1975 Reproduction, one bladed knife with opener on blade.
(stamped nickel panels) "Coca-Cola Co., Atlanta, Ga." stamped
on blade. $12.00

3. c.1983 Reproduction, similar to 1. at left, (cast brass side panels)
"Coca-Cola Co., Japan" stamped on blade. This knife was sold in
box with knife printed on box. $8.00

2. c.1975 Reproduction 2 blade knife with
hooked blade, (stamped brass panels)
"Coca-Cola Co., Atlanta, Ga.," stamped on
blade. "Germany" ink stamped on blade. $15.00

4. c.1985 Reproduction, 2 blade knife with
hooked blade (cast brass panels) "Utica
Stainless" and "Markatron Inc., Japan"
stamped on blade. $8.00

5. c.1985 Reproduction (not pictured) single blade plus opener/screwdriver
blade. (cast brass panels) "Gusstahl Solingen" stamped on blade. . . . $10.00

NOTE: Knives 1 and 2 were first to appear in the 1970's, there side panels were stamped with newly cut dies paterned after the original knives.
There are many very minor variations in the leave and vine designs when compared to the original knives. Knives 3,4, and 5 are actually reproductions of knives 1 and 2, showing the same minor variations. Knives 3,4, and 5, appear to have cast side panels, and are not as sharp in detail as knives 1 and 2.
Through the years, many collectors have been fooled by these knives, including myself. A little wear or simulated aging and rust can be deceiving. But knowing what is stamped on these blades and what is stamped on the originals, plus knowing the type of opener blades on the originals, you should be able to positively determine whether a knife is an original or reproduction. Refer to the "Pocket Knife" section of this book for blade stamping of original knives.
A special thanks to Thom Thompson of Versailles, Ky. for his research on this and for providing the photos and text.

-310-

FANTASY AND REPRODUCTIONS
POCKET MIRRORS

1973 Reproduction (oval) Pocket Mirrors .. . . . $2.00 Each
These were distributed by The Coca-Cola Co., There is a lesser quality copy of these that I consider worthless.

NOTE: All mirrors shown on this page (except oval reproductions) are "Fantasy Mirrors". This is only a small sampling of the many I've seen over the years. Keep in mind these mirrors are very easy to make and I consider them all worthless junk.

TRAYS (Recent, Repro, & Fantasy)

> **NOTE:**
> Repro: a tray reproduced to look like the original.
>
> Fantasy: a recently made tray that never existed as an original.
>
> Recent: a tray made within the last 10 or 12 years. Commemorative or special event trays.

1969 Lillian Nordica $25.00

1971 Repro (flat type) . . . $10.00

1970's (1917 Repro) . . $10.00

Repro: "Reg. US Pat. off" under logo
Original: Trade Mark in the tail of "C"

1970's (1914 Repro) $10.00

Repro: "Reg. US Pat. off" under logo
Original: Trade Mark in tail of "C"

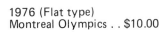

1976 (Flat type)
Montreal Olympics . . $10.00

1976 Indiana University . $5.00

1970's (Fantasy) . . . $5.00

CONDITION GUIDES

The condition of any Coca-Cola collectible is the most important factor in determining it's value. The "Mint" "Near Mint" form of grading items is the most commonly used. Keep in mind and certainly point out to dealers that "as the condition goes down, so does the value".

M	**MINT CONDITION**	New condition, unused, flawless, no visible marks or scratches.
NM	**NEAR MINT CONDITION**	Very minor or slight marks, a minor tear, nothing serious.
E	**EXCELLENT CONDITION**	Visible minor scratches, perhaps minor chips or marks, possibly some tears, still very collectible.
G	**GOOD CONDITION**	Scratches, minor flaking, possibly dents and rust or pitting, tearing, or peeling of paper items. An OK item.
F	**FAIR CONDITION**	More than minor pitting and flaking, trimmed or torn paper. A good filler item.
P	**POOR CONDITION**	In worn state, rusted, dented, or pitting, fadded, generally not in such hot shape.
R	**REPRODUCTION OR REISSUE**	An item that has been remade as a collectible item.
	FANTASY	A Fantasy item is a recently produced piece that never existed as an original advertising item.

Fantasy items have very little, if any, value.

TIPS FOR THE COLLECTOR

COLLECTING COCA-COLA — GENERAL OR SPECIALIZED

There seems to be many reasons why people enjoy collecting Coca-Cola memorabilia. Surely one of the greatest attractions is the wide range of collectibles available. There are many different areas of collecting, but most collectors will collect anything with the famous Coca-Cola logo. Others are specialized collectors. Because of the expense involved, it may be difficult for one collector to amass a great collection encompassing all areas. But, that same collector could have a fantastic collection in one specific area. Collecting only Coca-Cola bottles, for example, is a hobby enjoyed by many. Others may have set a goal to have every tray or calendar the company had produced. But when trying to track down items from the early or pre-1900's, they suddenly realize that it is quite a task.

One of my favorite specialized areas of collecting and one that even the new collector can get into without spending a fortune is postcards. Any postcard showing a nice Coca-Cola sign is a very good item. Postcards are easy to find and early ones are very desirable. But whether you collect anything and everything or specialize you always have a good feeling when you add a nice piece to your collection.

KEEP A RECORD

It is extremely important to keep an accurate and up-to-date record of each and every piece in your collection. Many people do not realize that you're not just collecting, but also, investing. Every piece that you spend money on or trade for is an investment that must be recorded. Could you imagine putting money in a bank without having a bank book recording the date, amount and interest. Well, the same holds true with money spent on your collection. If you have a computer, like so many people do, it is a terrific way to store all of this information. If a computer is not available to you go to your stationery store and buy a good hardbound record book. In it, list every piece, the date of purchase, amount paid, the condition and any other information you may want about the piece. You may want to keep things such as trays, calendars, toys, etc., separate to find them easier. If you sell or trade a piece, take note of the amount that you received for it.

If you have been collecting for sometime and haven't done this, do so as quickly as possible. Listing each and every item is a big job, I grant you, but believe me it should be done. This is very important also if you decide to sell your collection or perhaps leave it to a spouse or children. Remember, an up-to-date recording is the backbone of every collection.

INSURANCE

Not being an insurance agent or knowing your collection, I could not begin to tell you how to insure it. But I can give you some hints. One thing to remember is, do not assume that your collection is covered on your homeowners policy. Don't assume anything when it comes to insurance. Call your agent, invite him into your home or apartment, show him what you collect and get his advice. If you are not happy with what your agent tells you, call another and another

if necessary until you find a policy that you feel comfortable with.

There seems to be a number of ways to insure a collection, but which ever of these you choose be sure that it is insured some way. The agent may recommend that you increase your homeowners policy by adding a rider to it which will include the collection. Also inquire about a "Fine Arts" policy to cover some of the more expensive items.

You may be required to keep a photographic record of your collection for your insurance company. This, by the way is something that I recommend whether it is required or not. Try to set a minimum value of the items which are to be photographed.

FAKES AND REPRODUCTIONS

It's unfortunate but true; fakes and repros are a part of collecting. Whether it be Coca-Cola, Ming vases or Teddy Bears, reproductions are everywhere. The trick is to keep your mistakes to a minimum, and the best way to do that is plain and simple "education." Read everything you can get your hands on and ask questions. Put your mistakes behind you and learn from them. Also, tell other collectors about items that you know are phoney.

In this book you will find a number of pages devoted to fakes and repros. Remember, though, even with the many pieces shown it is still only a small sampling of the new, repro, and just plain junk that is passed off as old and original. Finding out if a piece is original or reproduction is important but questioning the dealer is not always the answer. They all seem to say the same thing, "We got this from a woman who had it in a trunk for the last fifty years." Don't be fooled by appearance. Many pieces can be instantly aged by unscrupulous dealers who are looking to make a buck from the collector who is anxious to make a major find.

I wish that there was some perfect way to know the repro from the original, but there isn't. I suggest seeing the original, holding it in your hands and feeling it. In many cases this is the best and surest method of not getting burnt.

RESTORING, CLEANING AND PRESERVING

Of all of the tips one can give to the collector this is certainly the most delicate. Can you imagine someone telling you how to clean and polish a tray, having you try it only to find that you have totally destroyed it. Well, believe me it's happened many times, especially with trays and metal signs.

My rule of thumb is, outside of simple dusting, leave the piece along unless you know exactly what you are doing. Some collectors have been very successful with dirt removal, cleaning and polishing, but many of them have learned through trial and error. This is certainly another area where education and asking questions is very important.

Touching up trays or signs is also a very sticky subject. It should never be done without a complete knowledge of what you are doing. Keep in mind that a tray that has been touched up, whether or not it is a good job, does not have the same value as a piece which has not been touched up. Many times a touched up piece is difficult to sell.

As far as paper is concerned the same rules apply. Do not do anything unless you know what you are doing. I do strongly recommend, however, protecting those paper items in an album or in a frame, especially calendars. And finally, always choose a frame shop that is knowledgeable in paper preservation and uses acid free matt board.

BUYING AT AN AUCTION

Auctions are great sources of Coca-Cola collectibles because they display some excellent artwork. Many pieces were saved and do turn up at house sales and auctions. Be sure to subscribe to mail auctions and antique publications, and make sure that you are aware of sales in and out of your area. Many auction houses will accept absentee bids, don't be afraid to ask and to use your phone. It can save you a lot of wasted time. I can't tell you how many miles I have traveled to auctions because a creative auctioneer listed in his advertisement "very rare Coke tray" only to find a 1950 tray that looked as if it had been run over by a truck. On the other hand though, I took a six hour trip to an auction that listed a Coke sign which turned out to be one of the most important pieces that I have ever purchased. Those pieces are the ones that make it all worth while.

Get to know your local auctioneers. If you feel that you trust them, let them know what your interests are. Believe me, the next time that they have a Coke piece, they will let you know about it. If a piece is listed in the advertisement, make a call, ask for a description and the condition. Go to the sale preview but don't run right up to the piece. Look at other items first and try not to be over anxious. Another tip is to, as difficult as it may be, try to set a limit as to what you will spend.

Many great Coke pieces have sold at auctions far below their value because they just didn't have the right audience. Yet, many pieces have sold far above their value because the right group of people were in the room.

CONSIDER CONDITION

As I have mentioned many times before, condition is the most important factor in determining the value of an item. That is why it is so difficult to put a value on an item in a book such as this. People, very often, do not consider condition. This is a major mistake. The prices that you see in this book are what I call "average prices," considering the item is in nice condition. If the piece is in mint condition the value is obviously higher and if it is in poor condition the price is of course lower. The price should always reflect the piece's condition.

It would be an error to purchase a piece for let's say $50.00 because it is in the price guide for $50.00 but the condition is poor. You should point out, to the dealer, any flaws in the piece and the price should be adjusted accordingly.

I, personally, have always been in favor of the "up-grade"

system of collecting. This is, basically, buying a piece and when you find the same piece in better condition, up-grade and sell the lesser of the two. Keep in mind that selling pieces in poor condition is not easy in many cases. So, before you turn your money over to a dealer, ask yourself this important question: "Am I considering condition in the purchase of this piece?"

GET INVOLVED

Join clubs and local chapters of those clubs, and become acquainted with other collectors and dealers. Read books, go to shows and auctions and of course, ask questions. Find out what pieces were recently found and how much they sold for. Know the market and remember that an informed and knowledgeable collector is a good collector. It is he who will eventually end up with a good collection. I can't tell you how many times I've heard things like "I've been collecting for years and I thought I was the only one" and "I had no idea that this stuff was worth this much." The more you know about the subject, the better off you will be.

I feel that it is so important to join a group such as the "Coca-Cola Collectors Club International" (an application can be found at the end of this book). Not only because it's a great group of people with a common interest, but it is, also, a great source of information to help you and your collection. Coca-Cola collectors have what many others don't. That is the tremendous support system of the Club. So, take advantage of it. Find out who specializes in a particular area ask questions if you need to. You will be surprised at how many collectors are willing to help. And, if at all possible try to attend at least one of the national conventions held by the Club. Getting to meet and talk to some knowledgeable collectors is a wonderful experience that you will never forget.

HELP FINANCE YOUR COLLECTION

Over the past ten or twelve years, I've seen the prices of Coca-Cola collectibles rise constantly and unless you have just hit the lottery or you are independently wealthy, it can be very difficult to amass a nice collection. But there are ways to help finance your collection as long as you are willing to spend some money.

I have heard many pople say that they have passed up worth while pieces because they have them in their collection. This is a mistake. If you are at a show and see an item that you feel is priced right you should buy it, even if you have it or if it is in a different area than your collection. You can sell it for a profit or use it for trade.

Another good way to make money is to put out a list of items for sale, up-grade items or duplicates. Advertise in the club newsletter. Let other collectors know that you have a list of items for sale. (Remember to keep close track of what you pay for items and what you sell them for.) Soon you will have a little nest egg for when you want to purchase that piece for your collection that always seemed to cost a fortune.

BOOKS ON THE SUBJECT

The following books are most helpful to the collector of Coca-Cola memorabilia. It is unfortunate that many of them are out of print, and sometimes difficult to locate. We have however seen them turn up in out dated book stores, flea markets, and from other collectors.

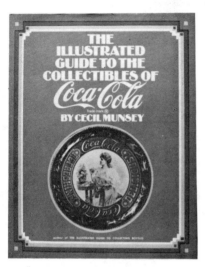

The Illustrated Guide to the Collectibles of Coca-Cola by Cecil Munsey 1972 Hawthorn Books, N.Y.

Soda Pop, by Lawrence Dietz 1973 Simon and Schuster

Coca-Cola An Illustrated History
by Pat Watters
1978 Doubleday & Co.

The Schmidt Museum Collection
Full Color, Hardbound
$33.95 + $3.00 Postage
To: Museum Book
Coca-Cola Bottling Co.
P.O. Box 647
Elizabethtown, Ky. 42701

The Wonderful World of Coca-Cola
by Martin Shartar and Norman Shavin
Color and B/W photos.

The Big Drink: The Story of Coca-Cola
by E.J. Kahn, Jr. 1960 Random House

The Chronicle of Coca-Cola Since 1886
1973 The Coca-Cola Co., Atlanta, Ga.

The Coca-Cola Company: An Illustrated Profile
1974 The Coca-Cola Co., Atlanta, Ga.

SCHMIDT'S *Coca-Cola* MUSEUM

ELIZABETHTOWN, KY.

The Schmidt Museum contains the world's largest private collection of Coca-Cola memorabilia. Since 1886, through the many years that Coca-Cola has been dispensed, bottled and canned, advertisement of the product has been of great importance. Items such as trays, calendars, glasses, leather goods, jewelry, dishes, playing cards, knives, toys, fans, book covers, sheet music, ashtrays and bottles, large and small, are some of the familiar every day objects prominently marked with the familiar script trademark. Unexpectedly, the trademark also appears on cigar bands, candy boxes, chewing gum, hand axes, coffee cups and silverware. Examples of all of these and more are displayed in the collection which covers more than 95 years of Coca-Cola advertising.

The visitor is taken back in time to reflect on the fashion and way of life during the period of the evolution of Coca-Cola. An 1890's soda fountain, complete with tin ceiling, hanging Tiffany lamp and elaborate stained glass dispensers is a special exhibit in the museum. In another area a three foot tall Tiffany Coke bottle shows its ruby light. The most complete collection of Coca-Cola trays known to exist highlights an entire wall and draws several thousand visitors each year.

The Schmidt Museum is located in the Coca-Cola Bottling Company in Elizabethtown, Kentucky. The Schmidt family has been producing Coca-Cola in Kentucky since 1901 and the third and fourth generation of the family are now responsible for the modern, up-to-date facility which is open to the public. In the lobby, a large pool filled with Japanese Carp reflects the many colors of the very large stained glass mural placed behind it. As the visitor leaves the lobby to enter the museum, he moves along a gallery to watch the modern bottling and canning procedures. After the many thirst provoking sights in the museum, the visitor finds the free ice cold Coke provided him, a very welcome touch.

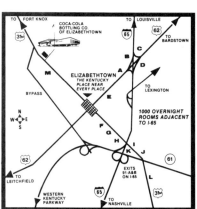

The Schmidt Coca-Cola Memorabilia Museum is open Monday through Friday from 9:00 a.m. to 4:00 p.m.

Closed every Saturday and Sunday, New Year's Day, Memorial Day, Fourth of July Labor Day, Thansgiving and Christmas.

ADMISSION

ADULTS $1.50
SENIOR CITIZEN (60 and over) . 1.00
STUDENTS 50

CHILDREN UNDER 6 FREE

(502) 737-4000

APPLICATION FOR MEMBERSHIP

Not sponsored by The Coca-Cola Company. Trade-marks used with permission.

The Coca-Cola Collectors Club International (formerly The Cola Clan) is a non-profit organization for collectors (and their families) who are interested in the history and the memorabilia of The Coca-Cola Company.

The Coca-Cola Collectors Club International provides:

- International communication among nearly 6000 collectors
- Markets for buying, trading and selling collectibles
- Informative monthly newsletter with free classified ads for members
- Special monthly merchandise offerings for members
- Regional chapters
- Annual international and regional conventions
- Yearly membership directory

Annual dues for primary membership in the United States, Canada and Mexico are **$15.00** (in U.S. dollars). Additional members of your family or organization may join as associates to your primary membership for **$5.00** per year (an associate member receives all the same benefits of membership as listed above except for the publications of the club). The dues for overseas primary membership are **$30.00** (in U.S. dollars) and includes **AIRMAIL** postage for the club's newsletter.

The Coca-Cola Collectors Club is not sponsored by The Coca-Cola Company, and is run by unpaid volunteers elected annually from the membership by mail ballot (all primary and associate members may run for elective office).

If you would like to join, complete the form below and return along with one year's dues to:

The Coca-Cola Collectors Club International
PO Box 546
Holmdel, NJ 07733

PLEASE PRINT	DUES
NAME (PRIMARY MEMBER)_____	**$15.00**
ADDRESS _____	($30.00 overseas)
CITY_____ **STATE** _____ **ZIP CODE** _____	
PHONE NUMBER (___) _____ area code	
NAME (ASSOCIATE MEMBER) _____	**$5.00**
(Give ADDRESS & PHONE if different from primary's)	
NAME (ASSOCIATE MEMBER) _____	**$5.00**
TOTAL AMOUNT ENCLOSED _____	